Communication
Best Practices at Dell,
General Electric,
Microsoft,
and
Monsanto

SUNY Series, Human Communication Processes
Donald P. Cushman and Ted J. Smith III, editors

Communication
Best Practices
at Dell,
General Electric,
Microsoft,
and Monsanto

by

Donald P. Cushman
and
Sarah Sanderson King

With a chapter by
Ted J. Smith III and William C. Adams

STATE UNIVERSITY OF NEW YORK PRESS

Published by
State University of New York Press, Albany

For information, address State University of New York Press,
90 State Street, Suite 700, Albany, NY 12207

Production by Marilyn P. Semerad
Marketing by Michael Campochiaro

Library of Congress Cataloging-in-Publication Data

Cushman, Donald P.
    Communication best practices at Dell, General Electric, Microsoft, and
    Monsanto / by Donald P. Cushman and Sarah Sanderson King ; with a
    chapter by Ted J. Smith III and William C. Adams.
        p. cm. — (SUNY series, human communication processes)
    Includes bibliographical references and index.
    ISBN 0-7914-5739-7 (alk. paper)—ISBN 0-7914-5740-0 (pbk. : alk. paper)
        1. Communication in organizations. 2. Benchmarking (Management)
    I. King, Sarah Sanderson, 1932– II. Title. III. SUNY series in human
    communication processes

HD30.3 .C876 2003
658.4'5—dc21   2002029184

10 9 8 7 6 5 4 3 2 1

We dedicate this book to each other.

Eighteen years of research underpin this book and the collaboration effort it fostered. This project was an adventure, a challenge and an education regarding the central role communication best practices plays in establishing quality relationships between people and organizations.
This book is thus dedicated to the relationship communication best practices fostered between its authors and the growth in knowledge, respect and insight such a collaboration guarantees.

Contents

Preface

In 1984, the University of Hawaii, East-West Center in Honolulu, and Harvard University provided research grants and/or support to begin an inquiry into the criteria high-tech firms employed in site selection. Armed with letters of introduction from Harvard University, we began interviewing the top management of high-tech firms located in Silicon Valley, California, the Highway 128 Beltway in Massachusetts, and the Research Triangle in North Carolina. From these interviews emerged the broad outline of what would become the theory of High-Speed Management, a new organizational communication theory.

Between 1984 and 2001, we had the opportunity to continue this line of research while consulting with over sixty firms and governments in Europe, Asia, and the Americas. We also were invited to report and update our research in MBA programs sponsored by ABB (formerly known as Asea Brown Boveri) and Siemens. In addition we held ten international conferences on High-Speed Management in Europe, Asia, and the United States. In 1994, the European International Business Association held its conference on High-Speed Management and we were invited to participate in that conference.

In 1998, our theory of High-Speed Management was named a finalist in the Arizona State University Organizational Communication Prize lecture contest for developing an original theory capable of stimulating and integrating the research in organizational communication. This line of research has generated over ten books and 50 chapters in books and journal articles.

This book is, then, the culmination of 18 years of research, training, consulting, and thoughtful analysis. We believe that this line of research has generated three important outputs: (1) an understanding of one appropriate method, the benchmarking of communication best practices, for researching the critical success factors involved in effective organizational communication; (2) an understanding of one method for developing a theory of organizational communication which has generality and necessity at the theoretic and practical levels of communication; and (3) an original and powerful theory of organizational communication High-Speed Management which can integrate organizational communication research and generate new lines of inquiry.

Donald P. Cushman
Sarah Sanderson King
November 2002

1

The Benchmarking of Organizational Communication Best Practices

Benchmarking is a process in which companies target key improvement areas within their firms, identify and study the best practices by others in these areas, and implement new processes and systems to enhance their own productivity and quality. Many leading companies are finding that in today's market, you benchmark and improve or you don't survive.

(Kendrick, 1992:1)

While leading-edge organizations have long understood and valued the benchmarking of best practices as a firm's most important theoretical and practical learning tool (Port et al. 1992, 75; Taylor 1999, 1), the field of communication has only recently begun to pursue this strategy as an important learning tool (King and Cushman 1994, 1995, 1997). Benchmarking the organizational communication patterns involved in the best practices of leading-edge firms benefits us as a strategic tool by (1) identifying the critical success factors in each area studied; (2) providing clear quantitative and qualitative targets to shoot for in developing world-class performance; (3) creating an awareness of state-of-the-art content, implementing structures, and processes for effective communication; and (4) mapping the learning curve for continuous improvement processes within organizations (Altany 1990, 14).

This book is one attempt to provide just such a knowledge base as a platform for understanding the organizational communication patterns involved in world-class performances. Our inquiry into the discovery of such patterns will proceed at both a theoretical and practical level by locating firms which by the consensus of experts manifest best practices (that is, world-class performances) in the areas of central concern to the development of communication theory and then employing the case studies method for benchmarking their performance.

Benchmarking as a significant learning tool is grounded in three important assumptions:

- that someone recognizes an insufficiency in his or her knowledge base regarding the theory and practice governing specific organizational communication activities;

- that someone knows of an organization which has and is willing to share its best practices knowledge base;

- that the person or persons recognizing the knowledge base insufficiency have the learning capability and implementation skills necessary to understand and implement the new knowledge base regarding best practices.

The benchmarking of organizational communication best practices takes place in three general areas of organizational concern.

First, Strategic Benchmarking seeks to discover the success various general communication strategies have in creating long-term stakeholder value. This is determined by measuring the effects of such strategies on a firm's growth in sales, profits, market share, productivity, quality, inventory turns, motivation, and customer satisfaction.

Second, Organizational Process Benchmarking seeks to discover one or more of a firm's primary communication processes on the previously listed stakeholder outcome measures. Here such communication processes with stockholders, suppliers, and employees are explored in order to reveal world-class best practices.

Third, Customer Benchmarking involves discovering the attributes which guide customer products or service choice, what firms are perceived to have these attributes, and which support services are needed to provide effective use of a product or service. This involves the benchmarking of organizational marketing, sales, and service communication processes and their effects upon organizational performance.

In order to understand the value of the benchmarking of best practices as a learning tool, this inquiry will employ strategic, process, and customer benchmarking studies of organizational communication best practices.

While 90 percent of the firms leading their respective market segments in the *Fortune Magazine International 500 Survey* attribute major portions of their competitive success to the benchmarking of best practices (Port et al. 1992, 75), several recent studies conducted in Europe, Asia, and the Americas report that 70 percent of all firms who attempt to benchmark best practices do not succeed (Kendrick

1992, 1). Such firms invest lots of time and money but fail to achieve their strategic objectives in their implementation. These studies suggest three primary factors which lead to a decline in performance after the benchmarking of organizational best practices:

First, a firm's learning capability. An insightful study undertaken by Ernst and Young and the American Quality Foundation documents the relationship between a firm's learning capability measures and its ability to employ teamwork and benchmarking effectively. Only the firms with the highest learning skills could employ the benchmarking of best practices effectively (Port et al. 1992, 66–70).

Second, a firm's timeline for acquiring and implementing the benchmarked best practices. Most firms undertake the benchmarking of best practices due to competitive pressures. Frequently insufficient time is allowed for the successful completion of the benchmarking processes. A firm must be able to survive the competitive pressures of other firms and still have time to learn and implement its best practices benchmarking.

Third, a firm's corporate culture. When a firm has a dramatically different corporate culture from the firm being benchmarked, considerable evidence exists that the firm doing the benchmarking finds it difficult to change its culture rapidly in order to accommodate the best practices observed. This in turn impedes the effectiveness of implementing the best practices.

In order to understand the constraints a firm's learning capabilities, corporate culture, and timelines place on the effective use of the benchmarking of best practices, this inquiry will investigate one example of each of these constraints on a firm.

Our examination of the value of benchmarking organizational communication best practices will therefore be divided into three parts: *Part 1 will benchmark the best practices of four firms:* the Dell Computer Corporation employing strategic benchmarking, General Electric and the Monsanto Company employing process benchmarking of the leadership and annual reports communication processes, and Microsoft employing customer benchmarking. *Part 2 will explore three limiting factors in effectively implementing organizational best practices*—organizational learning, time, and culture—in three firms: IBM, the Danville Bumper Works, and ABB. *Part 3 will explore the significance of the backbone organizational communication processes* which underlie the critical success factors and targets found in benchmarking studies.

Part 1 of our inquiry contains four benchmarking case studies of the organizational communication patterns involved in world-class best practices. A quality benchmarking inquiry into each of these four firms will proceed in five stages: (1) locating the core organizational process to be benchmarked; (2) identifying a firm whose communication patterns in regard to core organizational processes is considered an example of world class-best practices; (3) identifying the critical success factors for these organizational patterns; (4) articulating the key quantitative and qualitative targets for meeting the identified critical success factors; and (5) highlighting the unique backbone communication processes which underpin such world-class performances.

Chapter 2. Best Practices at the Dell Computer Corporation: Benchmarking a High-Speed Management Communication System. High-Speed Management is a general organizational communication strategy based on two propositions. *First,* reducing the cycle time an organization takes in getting its products or services to market relative to its competitors increases a firm's productivity, quality, market share, and profits, as well as its stakeholder and customer satisfaction with the firm. *Second,* improving an organization's communication processes by eliminating bottlenecks, speeding up information flow, and so forth is the most significant ingredient for reducing organizational cycle time.

The Dell Computer Corporation has developed a High-Speed Management communication system for dealing directly with its customers, suppliers, and workers which has improved the quality of organizational communication and cuts its cycle time in such a dramatic fashion as to endanger the viability of all its chief competitors, namely Compaq and IBM. Benchmarking the quality and speed of communication in this rapid-response system yields several remarkable critical success factors as well as quantitative and qualitative targets. For example, Dell takes customized computer orders over the Internet, its suppliers deliver parts for the order in 15 minutes, and Dell builds the computer in 3 hours and delivers it to the customer within 3 days. These rapid-response systems are placing pressure on Dell's chief competitors, causing them to lose money and market shares, to withdraw from the market, and to seek combinations with other firms not in Dell's market. Dell is continuously improving these rapid-response timelines by 20 percent per year, placing increased pressure on its competitors and threatening their survival.

Perhaps even more significant, this Internet rapid-response system has created five backbone communication processes which make the quality of Dell's communication so customer, worker, manager, and supplier adapted that it creates a significant advantage over its competitors. These backbone communication process include—(1) customer, (2) product, (3) value chain, (4) maintenance, and (5) continuous-improvement profiles. The Dell Computer Corporation provides strong support for High-Speed Management theory and reveals the specific implementing structures which make this theory so powerful in message construction and adaptation for coordinating organizational behaviors in the PC market.

Chapter 3. Best Practices at the General Electric Company: Benchmarking a World-Class Leadership Communication System. Organizational leadership is a foundational communication process. In the late 20th and early 21st centuries, leadership has become a study in how to successfully take a firm through rapid and repeated organizational change within the competitive environment created by a global economy. The General Electric Company is considered one of the best performing multinationals in the world. In 2001, GE was named *Fortune's* "Most Admired Company" for the fifth year in a row and was named The World's Most Respected Company by the *Financial Times* for the fourth time (GE Annual Report, 2001). Jack Welch, the CEO of GE, was considered one of the world's most effective leaders. In 1999, Jack Welch was named by *Fortune* as the Leader of the Decade, while the *Financial Times* and *Chief Executive Magazine* named Welch the most effective leader in the world. More significantly, over thirty of GE's former top executives have become successful CEOs of major global corporations. This suggests that GE's leaders and Jack Welch's leadership style have been principled, systemic, and teachable, rather than a function of Welch's unique abilities.

Our benchmarking case study of Welch's leadership system will locate the critical success factors and qualitative and quantitative targets employed in leading GE through three separate transformations. *The first change* involves transforming GE into the most competitive (i.e. profitable) and the most valued (i.e. capitalized) firm in the world. In order to achieve this vision, GE's eleven businesses were positioned in high-growth, high-margin businesses where GE could be number 1 or 2 in market shares. *The second change* involves transforming GE into a boundaryless firm based on speed, simplicity, and self-confidence. In order to achieve this vision, GE put in place a new corporate infrastructure, namely a new corporate culture, a new rapid-response corporate communication system, and a new continuous improvement system. *The third change* was the transformation of GE into a multipolar, multicultural Internet service firm which acts as a dominant force in Europe, Asia, and the Americas.

Perhaps even more significant, these successful transformations revealed a *backbone leadership communication process* involving five distinct stages: (1) locating and articulating a significant threat confronting the firm; (2) developing and articulating a clear vision for responding to that threat; (3) setting clear quantitative and qualitative targets for implementing that vision; (4) putting in place a state-of-the-art implementing structure for creating and releasing the tensions necessary to motivate change; and (5) empowering point people to lead and participate in the change. These organizational communication patterns of leadership allowed GE to significantly outperform all of its competitors and become recognized as developing a pool of world-class leaders.

Chapter 4. Best Practices at the Microsoft Corporation: Benchmarking a World-Class Marketing Communication System. Marketing is a foundational organizational communication process. The emergence of the Internet as a global e-marketing activity has changed dramatically the nature of global marketing, allowing very small firms, as we have seen in the Dell case study, to challenge very large firms in the global economy. This transformation in marketing strategy is creating a marketing revolution.

Microsoft is considered by most observers to be one of the most competitive firms in the marketing world. Lawrence Ellison, CEO of Oracle, a Microsoft competitor, argues that "Bill Gates and Microsoft do not just want to compete in the software industry. Rather, they seek to dominate every aspect of the market, to eliminate their competition" (Cortese et al. 1996, 86). Microsoft's marketing strategy has allowed it to gain a 92 percent market share in operating systems, a 98 percent market share in office applications, and a 72 percent market share in browser software. In addition, Microsoft's 50 percent profit margins are among the largest in the world (Nee 1999, 112). While Microsoft's competitors complain and several governments investigate the firm's monopolistic behaviors, the firm's strategic marketing techniques are being imitated by its global competitors and by firms in other industries.

Our benchmarking case study will examine Microsoft's attempts to pioneer and orchestrate mass markets at a time when the software market was shifting from PC to Internet activities. In so doing Microsoft employed five critical success factors in guiding their macro competitive activities: (1) enter evolving mass markets early or stimulate new markets with good products which can become the industry standard; (2) incrementally continuously improve products, periodically making old products obsolete; (3) push volume sales to ensure that products become and remain the industry standard; (4) leverage the industry standard to develop new products and market linkages; and (5) integrate, extend, and simplify products and services to reach new mass markets. These critical success factors and their qualitative and quantitative targets are tools for dominating competitors.

Perhaps even more significant are *Microsoft's backbone communication* processes for implementing its critical success factors. Thus Microsoft was able to forge specific types of communication linkages between (1) product development, continuous improvement programs, and Microsoft's unique brand of teamwork; (2) the setting of industrial standards, Microsoft's unique acquisitions, product development, and alliance policies; (3) the volume marketing; distribution, competitive pricing, exclusive contracting, and software bundling policies; and (4) the leveraging of software standards to limit competitors' sales while pushing Microsoft's new products into new mass markets. Explaining how these communication processes are being used to dominate the computer software market, the Internet browser and server markets, and now the information storage market is an insightful study into world-class marketing performance and indicates why Microsoft will be a dominant software firm regardless of the outcome of the government antitrust proceedings.

Chapter 5. Best Practices at the Monsanto Chemical Company: Benchmarking World-Class Annual Reports. This essay contributed by Drs. Ted J. Smith III and William C. Adams addresses another core organizational communication process, the patterns of communication involved in effectively addressing a firm's stockholders in annual reports. Traditionally, annual reports are divided into two sections. The front section allows a firm's top management to present its strategic plan—its business model—while addressing common themes regarding past performances and future expectations. The rear section presents the financial information required by the Securities and Exchange Commission and the New York Stock Exchange: The annual report is a company's primary calling card, the lasting visual impression of a company.

Monsanto's annual reports have been recognized nationally and internationally for their excellence, receiving 15 major awards of excellence from four different groups: *Institutional Investor Magazine*, the International Association of Business Communication, the National Investors Corporation, and *Financial World Magazine*. This focus group benchmarking study of Monsanto's annual report yields several critical success factors. Such reports must address up front (1) current sales, profits, stockholder values, operating margins, and one-time charges against profits as well as future expectations in these same areas; (2) future strategic directions and leadership changes; and (3) the current and future performance of key products and services. The targets employed in preparing the reports require utilizing instant comprehension in (1) the selection, repetition, and variation on a common set of themes; (2) placing those themes in a clear deductive framework; and (3) illustrating all key themes with simple, bright-colored visuals such as bar charts and contribution pies.

Perhaps more significant are the backbone communication processes in the annual report: (1) the use of a letter from a chairperson or CEO to highlight future expectations and current results; (2) the handling of negative information up front in a candid manner, listing clear corrective remedies in regard to the issues, followed by an optimistic discussion of future expectations in these areas; (3) a focus on future expectations and the specific plans made to make sure these expectations are met; and (4) the discussion of new strategies and business processes for increasing a firm's competitiveness. A firm's reputation and management credibility are measured by the manner in which the firm meets or exceeds positive future expectations and the annual report is the key document for establishing those expectations.

We have previewed in some detail the chapters contained in part 1 of this book, which deal with the benchmarking of best practices in High-Speed Management (Dell), leadership (GE), marketing (Microsoft), and annual reports (Monsanto). *Part 2* attempts to document three specific limiting factors—organizational learning, response time, and culture—to the successful implementation of organizational best practices. In each case we will examine the roots of the limitations and then employ a case study method to explore how these factors, if not handled appropriately, can impair the implementation of best practice processes.

Chapter 6. Organizational Learning as a Limiting Factor: A Case Study of IBM's PC Unit. We all recognize the fact that some individuals learn faster and have more operational skills than other individuals. Less obvious is the fact that the same holds true for firms. Ernst and Young, a consulting firm, conducted a global study into why some firms succeed while others fail in their attempts to implement the organizational benchmarking of best practices. What this study revealed was that some firms are capable of learning better and have more operationally skilled employees than other firms. More significantly Ernst and Young developed a method for measuring a firm's learning and performance capabilities. These measures can then be used to predict the types of continuous-improvement skills which different levels of learning capabilities allow a firm to employ successfully. According to these measures, only firms with the highest level of learning capabilities can employ the benchmarking of organizational best practices successfully. (Port et al. 1992, 66–67).

In 1996, IBM's PC unit benchmarked the Dell Computer Corporation's best practices in reducing cycle time in order to improve its competitiveness. IBM's PC unit attempted five times in four years to implement these best practices and failed each time. After each failure, IBM replaced its top management team in an effort to succeed. They even hired a top manager from Dell to lead the effort. Unfortunately years of downsizing and internal troubles had taken its toll on the PC unit's employees, with many of the best people moving on to other firms. In each of these five one-year time frames, IBM's employees failed the Ernst and Young learning criteria for successfully implementing the benchmarking of organizational best practices and in each year they failed at implementation, causing the IBM PC unit to lose $161 million, $39 million, $500 million, and $1 billion respectively. It is now clear that IBM must raise the general learning levels and skills of its PC unit employees or exit competing with Dell in the global PC market.

Chapter 7. Time as a Limiting Factor: A Case Study of the Danville Bumper Works. Most firms undertake the benchmarking of best practices in order to improve their own performance, to become more competitive. Seldom do they realize that the implementation of best practices may be very time consuming, even if the firm's employees are skilled and learn well. In such cases, a firm must be capable of remaining profitable for the length of time needed to learn and implement these best practices.

The Danville Bumper Works was confronted with just such a problem. This small firm wanted to provide Toyota with bumpers for its cars and trucks. It entered into a joint venture with Toyota to benchmark Toyota's best practices in producing bumpers. Then, under the mentorship of Toyota, it attempted a very long and difficult effort to implement these best practices. This process of benchmarking and then implementation of best practices began in 1980 and was completed in 1988. This case study documents the slow and somewhat arduous task of succeeding in the benchmarking process. The Danville Bumper Works was financially stretched during this eight-year time frame, but succeeded in the end. A firm must have the time and patience it takes to succeed in the benchmarking of best practices process, so quick results are not normally possible, as this case illustrates.

Chapter 8. Culture as a Limiting Factor: A Case Study of ABB. Regional, national, and organizational cultures prescribe behavioral patterns which are difficult and sometimes impossible for an organization to change. In many instances organizational best practices from one region, nation, or organization are not translatable into the practices of other regions, nations, or organizations without significant cultural costs. For example, it has taken Japanese organizations over ten years of constant pressure from competitors and three recessions to change their cultural commitments to lifelong employment. It has been an expensive lesson, one slowly learned, and the practice is now changing in only the most financially threatened firms. Yet years ago Japanese firms benchmarked how firms like GE and Ford responded to precipitous drops in sales by rightsizing their organizations and concluded it was culturally impossible to employ downsizing in Japan.

In 1993 ABB (formerly Asea Brown Boveri), an electrical engineering firm, decided to benchmark the best practices of the General Electric Company. Its reasons were simple. In an industry made up of such global competitors as Hitachi, Mitsubishi, and Toshiba from Asia; Siemens, ABB, and Alston from Europe; and GE from the Americas, GE made more profits in one year than all these other firms' profits taken together. What ABB found after one year of benchmarking was that (1) GE was a decentralized firm, while ABB was centralized; (2) GE produced only high margin niche products while ABB was a full-service provider; (3) GE had a clear global vision, specific quantitative targets, and a monitoring and penalty system for not meeting targets, while ABB had none of these; (4) GE fast-tracked competent young managers, while ABB stalled upward mobility due to a politically established hierarchy; and (5) GE had open competition in all markets between all units while ABB designated specified units only as having access to certain markets. For ABB to adopt GE's benchmarked best practices, it would have to abandon its stockholder system, management system, monitoring and reward system, marketing systems, and corporate strategy—in short, its organizational culture. By 1999, seven years after this benchmarking process, it was clear that ABB had not attempted to implement any of GE's best practices. To do so would call for reinventing the firm. However, in that seven-year period, GE's sales went from $50 to $111 billion, and profits from $4 to $10 billion. GE's European sales went from $10 to $40 billion and profit margins rose to near 30 percent. ABB's global sales in this same time frame went from $28 to $24 billion, its profits rose from $760 million to $1.6 billion, and its profit margins approached 7 percent. These figures were sufficiently embarrassing when compared with GE that ABB's CEO Goran Lindahl agreed in 1999 to head a second benchmarking study of GE undertaken by the Performance Group, an Anglo-Norwegian Consultancy (Burt 1999, 10). Whereas significant cultural barriers existed at ABB for understanding and utilizing its first benchmarking study, years of restructuring ABB under Lindahl's guidance had created a new culture which was more receptive to GE's best practices.

However, in 2001, before ABB could undertake significant change based on its second benchmarking of GE, two significant flaws in ABB's old culture pushed the company into organizational disarray. First, ABB's strong top-down culture allowed two former CEOs to set compensation packages which were extremely excessive without being reviewed. Second, this top-down culture led to the firm's acquisition of a U.S. firm without exercising due diligence, resulting in 90,000 civil lawsuits against ABB which will cost the firm billions of dollars. This in turn has led to a financial crisis at ABB and a change in the firm's top management team. This crisis, while delaying the implementation of best practices, now could accelerate the implementation of change in the next few years.

Part 3 of this book seeks to draw some conclusions from our inquiry. Our task is to summarize and integrate our findings in regard to locating critical success factors and the discovery of backbone communication processes which underlie the successful benchmarking of best practices.

Chapter 9. Backbone Communication Processes in the Benchmarking of Best Practices. Our inquiry in chapters 2 through 5 has isolated critical success factors for achieving the benchmarked best practices of highly successful firms. Such critical success factors appear to transcend time and place, forming individually necessary conditions and collectively sufficient conditions for successfully implementing best practices in the areas under consideration. The qualitative and quantitative targets for achieving the critical success factors appear to vary by time and place, based upon the performance of competitors.

Perhaps our most significant findings in each of these inquiries are specific backbone communication processes which in fact are the implementing processes which allow firms to achieve their targets and fulfill their critical success factors. These communication engines for success elaborate the foundational implementing processes for a new theory of organizational communication. High-Speed Management emphasizes effective performance and provides well-developed subtheories of message content, leadership communication, marketing communication, and communication with stockholders.

Let the adventure of looking inside the best practices of world-class firms begin, guided by the road map provided above.

References

Altany, D. (1990). Copycats, *Industry Week,* November 5, 11–18.

Altany, D. (1992). Benchmarkers unite. *Industry Week,* (February): 1–8.

Burt, T. (1999). All change for profit. *Financial Times,* June 29, 10.

Cortese, A., Verity, J., Rebello, K., and Hoff, R. (1996). The software revolution. *Business Week,* December 4, 75–90.

Cushman, D., and King, S. S. (eds.) (1995). *Communicating Organizational Change: A Management Perspective,* Albany: SUNY Press.

———. (1997). *Continuously Improving an Organization's Performance: A High-Speed Management Perspective,* Albany: SUNY Press.

———. (1999). Stimulating and integrating the development of communication research in High-Speed Management. *Management Communication Quarterly* 3 (November): 309–325.

Fuchsberg, G. (1992). Quality programs show shoddy results. *Wall Street Journal,* May 14, B1-B7.

Immelt, J. (2001). GE Annual Report, 1.

Kelly, K. (1985). An interview. *Financial Executive Magazine,* 34.

Kendrick, J. (1992). Benchmarking survey builds case for looking to others for TQM models. *Quality,* March, 1.

King, S. and Cushman, D. (eds.) (1994). *High-Speed Management and Organizational Communication in the 1990s: A Reader,* State University of New York Press.

Nec, E. (1999). Microsoft gets ready to play a new game. *Fortune,* April 26, 107–112.

Port, O., Cary, J., Kelly, K., and Forest, R. (1992). Quality. *Business Week,* November 30, 64.

Taylor, R. (1999). Making a nest for high-flyers. *Financial Times* November 15, 1.

Part 1

Benchmarking Foundational Communication Processes

A lot of companies are internally focused and have not thought about going outside the company to get information. Some of these managers are locked into the mentality of improving only on last year's performance by 10 percent, and don't realize that another company might be 100 percent or 1000 percent more efficient than they are in a certain function. By not identifying these areas and learning more efficient techniques, they remain behind. Company goals should always be geared towards being the best in the world, rather than just slightly better than last year.

(Sierk, 1990)

In **Part 1** we will benchmark the world class performance of four firms:

1. The *Dell Computer Corporation's* development of a world-class *rapid-response communication system* for interacting with all of a firm's stakeholders.

2. The *General Electric Company* for developing a world-class *leadership communication system* for turning out CEOs.

3. The *Microsoft Corporation* for developing a world-class *marketing and sales communication system* for satisfying customer needs.

4. The *Monsanto Company* for developing a world-class *annual report communication system* for communicating organizational value to investors.

2

Best Practices at the Dell Computer Corporation: Benchmarking a High-Speed Management Communication System

We're in a world that is obsessed with speed. "Time" has won the race to become our most valued resource.... Time to market, that is, the elapsed time between product definition and availability... is becoming a highly competitive issue for U.S. companies, and... it may be the single most critical factor for success across markets.... Speed to market creates opportunities in market share, market leadership, and profits.

(Versey, 1991:23-26)

Fraker, writing in *Fortune* described a new set of economic forces which were dramatically affecting organizational performance. These forces included (1) quick market saturation, (2) unexpected global competition, and (3) rapid technological breakthroughs. These forces taken collectively required a new management theory based on responding to rapid environmental change, shifting customer needs, and competitors' adaptation to those needs (Fraker 1984:62-68). Between 1984 and 1988 those economic forces gave rise to a new High-Speed Management Communication theory which focused on the use of computers, telecommunication, and extremely well-crafted messages to provide a rapid-response system adapted to customer needs and competitor products. Such a rapid-response system has placed pressure on research in organizational communication processes to more precisely and economically create message contents which were adapted to a specific audience and instantly intelligible. This new High-Speed Management Communication theory was presented in its most complete form by the authors in 1995 and 1997 and by Cullin and Cushman in 1999. High-Speed Management includes new, well-developed theories of environmental scanning, value chain performance, continuous-improvement programs, leadership, marketing, and teamwork programs.

High-Speed Management is a communication theory rooted in two philosophic and empirically verifiable propositions.

First, reducing the cycle time an organization takes in getting its products or services to market yields several significant outcomes. More specifically, decreasing organizational cycle time yields increases in productivity, quality, market shares, profits, management, worker motivation and commitment, and customer satisfaction (Versey 1991; Dumaine 1989). For example General Electric reduced the cycle time it takes to deliver a washer or dryer to market from three weeks to three days, saving millions of dollars and yielding all the above mentioned benefits (Stewart 1991, 119).

Second, improving an organization's communication processes is the most significant ingredient for reducing organizational cycle time (Cushman and King 1995). Removing communication bottlenecks, standardizing information transfer, developing rapid-response systems, and improving message quality and adaptation to all an organization's stakeholders are the central outputs that yield decreased organizational cycle time. For example, General Electric put in place a rapid-response communication system between customers and managers which reduced the cycle time GE took in responding to specific customer needs from four weeks to 7 days, saving GE millions of dollars while increasing customer satisfaction (Cushman and King 1995, 1997; Cullin and Cushman, 1999).

The purpose of this inquiry is to benchmark the Dell Computer Corporation and its top two competitors in the PC computer market in order to discover how Dell achieved dramatic success in cycle time reduction through improved organizational communication processes. Our benchmarking case study will proceed in four stages: (1) an examination of the competition in the personal computer market, (2) a benchmarking of Dell's rapid-response systems, (3) an examination of the effect of Dell's rapid-response systems on Dell's customers and competitors, and (4) the drawing of come conclusions regarding the benchmarking of Dell's reduced cycle times and High-Speed Management theory.

Competition in the Personal Computer Market

*Making PCs has become, is, and will continue to be a nasty
business. It is a business in which companies cut prices literally
every week, where the product you make is obsolete just
months after you make it, where customers choose between
your boxes and similar boxes made by several rivals.*

(Serwer, 1998:59)

The computer industry represents fertile ground for our inquiry. The
market is highly visible, rapidly growing, and competitive, with several
well-managed dynamic firms seeking increased market shares. In 1998,
the $148 billion computer market had four main segments: main frames,
minis, workstations, and personal computers. PC sales represented 46
percent of total computer sales. Table 2.1 tracks the performance of the
top three computer firms in market shares in the PC market between
1996 and 2001 utilizing data from *Data Quest* and *International Data.*

Table 2.1
PC Market Shares

	1st Quarter 1996	1st Quarter 1997	1st Quarter 1998	1st Quarter 1999	1st Quarter 2000	1st Quarter 2001
Compaq	10.0%	11.5%	13%	14%	13.8%	13.3%
IBM	7.2%	7.3%	7.5%	7%	6.5%	6.0%
Dell Computer	3.4%	5.3%	11.8%	15%	19%	24.9%

Source: *Data Quest,* 1996–2002; International Data, 1996–2002

Between 1996 and 2001, Compaq's sales growth was +30 percent, IBM's was –1.2 percent, and Dell's was +750 percent. However,
while market shares were increasing, average margins in the industry were decreasing from +10 to -10 percent.

The PC market has three major components: laptops, desktops, and servers. By November of 2001 Dell's rank and market
shares in each component of the U.S. PC market were number 2 in
laptops with 24 percent of the market, number 1 in desktops with
29 percent of the market, and number 5 in servers with 16 percent
of the market. This gave Dell 24.9 percent of the total PC market
and allowed Dell to pass Compaq as the number one producer of
PCs in the United States. Dell's financial performance over the past
six years is recorded in table 2.2.

Table 2.2
Dell's Six-Year Financial Performance Returns
(in billions of U.S. dollars)

	2001	2000	1999	1998	1997	1996
Sales	31.1	31.8	26	18.2	12.3	7.7
Profits	1.2	2.1	2	1.4	1.3	.7

Source: www.Dell.com Financial, 2, 2000:1

Dell Computer was and is the low cost, high value provider of PCs backed by world-class rapid-response, continuous-improvement, and service programs.

Benchmarking Dell Computer's Rapid-Response Communication System

Dell is a model cycle reduction time firm. Dell applies cycle reduction logic to every aspect of its operations with dramatic results.

(Serwer, 1998:62)

Dell Computer Corporation is one of the most visible success stories in the computer market. By selling personal computers directly to customers over the Internet, offering a build-to-order sales system, and then linking suppliers, workers, managers, customers, and service personnel together on the Internet Dell has built a series of rapid-response systems that have revolutionized organizational communication. Dell's rapid-response systems have led to fear, admiration, and attempts at imitation among its competitors and other e-businesses alike (McWilliams 1997, 132–136, 91–92; McWilliams and White 1999, 84).

Critical Success Factors

Dell employs four rapid-response systems. Each system uses the Internet to provide a real-time communication system for linking key organizational stakeholders together into a functional community. Each rapid-response system employs a backbone profiling system for precisely adapting the content of communication to each of an organization's stockholders. These profiles are then used to improve future communication and to maintain interpersonal relationships between stakeholders. This in turn enhances the firm's organizational performance. Individually, these four rapid-response systems are necessary conditions for rapid and successful organizational communication and collectively they represent sufficient conditions along with their accompanying targets for successful organizational performance (Margretta 1998, 73–83; Stepanek 1998, 51–52).

First, Dell has a rapid-response sales link to its customers. This interactive online communication system allows customers to order and track their purchase through each stage of the manufacturing and distribution process. Employing mail catalogs and Internet home pages, customers interact directly with Dell and can customize their orders to meet their unique needs. Since 1998, this includes an Internet Superstore with thirty thousand computer parts. This Superstore provides everything from different types of chips to different types of add-ons. These interactive communication processes arc tracked by Dell in order to build backbone customer and product communication profiles. The profiles of customer choice allow Dell to notify individuals of useful add-ons, key advances in technology, and new services which might meet the customer's previously indicated needs. The profile of product orders assists Dell in streamlining its value chain, dealing with suppliers, and monitoring product changes. In addition Dell offers customers online chat rooms for discussions with other customers, Dell managers, and Dell's maintenance staff. Once a week Dell hosts an online interactive lecture on various new advances in computer technology. These interactive communication processes help Dell maintain interpersonal relationships with its customers and to adapt its products rapidly to changing customer needs. The result is that Dell's laptop, desktop, workstation, and services have won awards as the top products in their classes in customer surveys conducted by *PC World,* Best Buy Stores, *Windows Magazine,* and *Fortune Magazine* (Ransted 1999, B1).

Second, Dell has a rapid-response system for providing customer service. This interactive real-time communication system can be accessed by telephone or computer for personal or automated technical and customer support in dealing with computer problems. This service is toll free 24 hours a day, seven days a week throughout the world in multiple languages. Dell monitors these service interactions in order to construct maintenance profiles on each piece of equipment and the appropriate instructions for its use, and to develop appropriate repair sequences for each type of problem for use by its live and automated repair processes. Such profiles allow Dell to warn customers of potential problems, develop clear problem correction routines, and access equipment and worker performance in manufacture and assembly. This interactive customer service system has won Dell awards from *Fortune Magazine*, *PC World Magazine*, *Windows Magazine*, and Best Buy Stores as the number one computer firm in customer service.

Third, Dell has a rapid-response system for linking all suppliers, workers, managers, and customers to Dell's value chain. This interactive real time communication system is employed to order parts, manufacture and outsource computer modules, and coordinate assembly and distribution of products to customers. Managers employ this system for all human resource functions, workers and suppliers for all coordination sequencing and quality control processes, and customers to track manufacturing and distribution processes. Dell monitors each of these activities and develops performance profiles and report cards for immediate feedback to suppliers, managers, and workers on their performances. The company conducts interactive online training and workshop programs to improve stakeholder skills and also utilizes chat rooms for advanced learning and team coordination activities. Dell's real-time communication system for value-chain coordination sets the standard for excellence in response time and product quality in the PC industry.

Fourth, Dell has a rapid-response system for the continuous improvement of all organizational activities. Here again, all Dell's stakeholders are tied together in a real-time interactive communication system aimed at focusing teamwork on improving every aspect of Dell's performance. Such teams operate with and between units, outsourcers, suppliers, and managers and customers, aiming to improve Dell's productivity, quality, maintenance, and timelines by at least 20 percent per year. Each of these teamwork processes is monitored and profiled in order to locate innovative and ambitious project leaders and effective team members and to motivate stakeholders (McWilliams and White 1999, B4). This continuous-improvement process leads the PC industry in improved performance each year.

Dell's four rapid-response systems—sales, services, value chain, and continuous improvement—are all online real-time communication systems. Dell's profiling systems of customer choice, products, service, value chain, and continuous-improvement performance track the content of focused interaction aimed at improving the organizational performance and make up the critical success factors in designing effective messages and products in Dell's direct sales model.

Benchmarking Targets

By 1998, Dell's aggressive pricing of products and rapid-response communication systems had begun to cut significantly into Compaq and IBM's market shares and reduced the profit margins of these firms to zero. In an effort to combat these trends a benchmarking study of all three firms was undertaken to reveal what could be done to combat Dell's advance. Table 2.3 contains the critical success factors and targets benchmarked.

First, in 1998, 43 percent of Dell's sales were made over the Internet, and 57 percent by telephone. By 1999, 60 percent of Dell's sales were made over the Internet and 40 percent by telephone. In 1998 this amounted to $10 million in Internet sales per day and grew

Table 2.3
Benchmarking the Competitiveness of the
Top 3 PC Firms in the U.S. Market

Critical Success Factors	Dell	Compaq	IBM
1. Customer sales			
Web sales	43%	10%	20%
Online customization	Yes	No	No
Computer to customer/online	3 days	12 days	15 days
Computer to customers/stores	0	35 days	30 days
Average retailer costs	0	20%	20%
Average sales incentives	0	$1000	$1000
Convert sales to cash	1 day	30 days	25 days
2. Customer service			
Online tech support	24 hrs.	8 hrs.	8 hrs.
Online service support	24 hrs.	8 hrs.	8 hrs.
Computer networks installed	14 days	60–90 days	60 days
Chat rooms	Yes	No	No
Interactive lectures	Yes	No	No
Customer service costs	Free	Paid	Paid
3. Value Chain			
Parts inventory average	15 min.	7–10 days	10 days
Computer inventory average	3 days	30 days	25 days
Produce computer average	4 hrs.	15 days	12 days
Computer to customer average	3 days	30 days	25 days
4. Continuous Improvement			
% upgrade per year	20%	10%	10%
% of stakeholders involved	100%	40%	40%

to $34 million by 1999. Ninety percent of Dell's sales were to institutions, 70 percent of which involve $1 million in orders each year. In addition, 10 percent or $1 billion of Dell's sales were to individuals (McWilliams 1999f, B4). In 1998 Dell was the only firm which could customize Internet PC sales. Direct electronic marketing allowed Dell to convert its sales to cash in one day. Marketing primarily through sales outlets, Compaq and IBM took an average 25 to 35 days from the day of sales at the outlet to receive payment. Compaq and IBM Internet sales were referred to sales outlets to fill orders. In addition these outlets held 35- to 120-day inventories before the sale of products. Since the dollar value of a computer drops at 1 or 2 percent per week, Compaq and IBM must pay retailers for weekly price erosions. In addition Compaq and IBM pay retailers a 20 percent commission on sales. When inventories in sales outlets reach beyond the 30-day limit, Compaq and IBM reduce the price of these computers through the use of sales incentives which average $1000 per unit and add to their outlet costs (Margretta 1998, 73–84). Dell thus achieves significant time, fit, and cost advantage from direct electronic sales to customers.

Second, Dell requires all component manufacturers for its PCs, with the exception of those who manufacture monitors, to warehouse their components within 15 minutes of Dell's various production plants. Computer monitors are mailed directly from SONY to customers and coordinated by FedEx so as to arrive at the same time as the computers for assembly. This allows Dell to save $30 in shipping costs per monitor. Compaq and IBM hold 7- to 10-day inventories of parts at manufacturing facilities and 25- to 120-day computer inventories at sales outlets, thus significantly increasing their inventory costs. Dell manufactures computers in 4 hours, Compaq and IBM in 15 and 12 days respectively, thus increasing their manufacturing costs. Dell gets a computer to its customers within 3 days, Compaq and IBM in 15 to 30 and 12 to 25 days respectively, thus increasing their distribution costs. Dell installs computer networks in 14 days, Compaq and IBM in 60 to 90 days, thus increasing their installation costs. Once again, Dell achieves a quicker, higher quality, lower price advantage over its competitors.

Dell can produce PCs at an average cost of 20 percent less than its competitors while retaining its 20 percent operating profit margins. This in turn allowed Dell to sell its PCs at 20 percent less than its competitors for comparable equipment, placing pricing pressures on its competitors. If Dell's competitors place their equipment price above that of Dell, they lose significant market shares. If they match Dell's lower prices they lose their profit margins and operate in the red.

Third, Dell's free customer service system is open 24 hours a day, seven days a week. It offers both human and automated support as well as free online interactive chat rooms, lectures, and technical and customer support. Its competitors offer limited eight-hour telephone support for which they charge. With most large customers, like Boeing, which has 100,000 Dell PCs, Dell puts 30 technicians on site and they function as part of Boeing's Information Technology program. For small firms, Dell outsources service contracts and service centers (Margretta 1998, 78). By the beginning of 1999 Dell began a new push to improve customer service by providing several online service links directly to customers. These new online services include a conversation between customers and Dell managers called "Dell Talk." This program focuses on customer relevant topics like the year 2000 problem and trends in PC and server development. In addition, a new net program called "Ask Dudley" employs advanced artificial intelligence software which will allow Dell technicians to answer hundreds of service questions on the Internet. Finally, Dell is introducing another Web server feature called "My Dell Web Pages," instructing users on the latest advances in customized home pages for its customers. Today one-third of Dell's customer service force is involved in handling online inquiries. Since each toll-free telephone call costs Dell an average of $25 per call, shifting customers to these new direct-link websites will save Dell thousands of calls per week and millions of dollars (Stepanek 1998, 52). Dell's continuous-improvement programs are reducing its costs at 20 percent per year while Compaq and IBM achieve 10 percent cost reductions. Dell involves all its firm's stakeholders in online real-time interaction to reduce costs while Compaq and IBM do not.

Fourth, Dell's use of such backbone communication content processes as customer, product, value chain, maintenance, and continuous-improvement profiles along with stakeholder report cards on performance allow Dell to communicate with its stakeholders in powerful ways not accessible to its competitors. This in turn led customers in a *PC World* survey of customer satisfaction to rank Dell number 1 (Stepaneck 1998, 52) and as the most admired among PC firms by its competitors (Serwer 1998, 60).

The Effect of Dell's Rapid-Response System on Its Customers and Competitors

*Speed kills—if you don't have it. Whether it's product develop-
ment, marketing, or customer service.*

(Elstrom, 1999:EB35)

Dell Computer's growth in sales, profits, market shares, and stock
price has been remarkable. Over the past six years, sales have
climbed from $5.2 billion to $32 billion (that is 50 percent com-
pounded annual growth). Profits are up from $300 million to $2 billion today (that's 80 percent annual growth). Dell's market shares
have tripled in the past five years to 24.9 percent. Since 1990, Dell's
stock has risen from 23 cents in 1990 to $29 per share, a rise of 1,000
percent (Dell Fact Sheet 2002). In 1998 Dell took its direct marketing
model for desktop computers into five new markets—laptops, servers, computers below $1000, large computer storage systems, and
the network market, extending its reach beyond PCs. By the end of
2001, Dell's world-wide growth was at 18 percent in servers while
Compaq was -17 percent in PCs and -4.9 percent in servers; IBM was
-11.7 percent in PCs and +.05 percent in servers (Daniel 2002, 18).

  To remain competitive with Dell in 1997 both Compaq and IBM
cut prices dramatically to match Dell. They both watched their PC
sales grow more slowly than Dell's. The result was that Compaq's
earnings decreased and IBM lost $161 million dollars. In 1998, with
Dell's sales growing, Compaq and IBM watched their inventories
grow to 120 days. Both firms began a price war in an attempt to
reduce inventories at outlets to 20 days in order to cut retailer
costs. One result of this price war was that Compaq and IBM saw
their 1998 PC profits drop dramatically. Compaq's profits dropped
from a projected $510 million to $16 million even though sales grew
38 percent. On April 18, 1999, Compaq's CEO and CFO were forced
to resign (Kehoe 1999, 21). In 1998 IBM's PC unit lost market shares
and went $992 million in the red and the CEO of its PC unit was
forced to resign (Kirkpatrick 1998).

Compaq's PC Strategy

Compaq's continuous-improvement program had slowed in 1998-1999.
New, more competitive targets were introduced by management that
aimed at revitalizing and improving the program. At the same time,

Compaq had decided to cut its prices again in order to become more competitive in the price war with IBM. Compaq, seeing its competitive disadvantage vis-à-vis IBM, namely IBM's larger service force and the ability to spread its escalating PC costs across all its other profit areas and still make money, decided to acquire the Digital Equipment Company. This would allow Compaq to move into the data storage, work station, mini, and mainframe markets, where margins were larger than in PCs. It also would allow Compaq to significantly bolster its service staff, the fastest growing and highest margin area in the computer industry (Hansell 1999, B1). By 2002 with Compaq's market shrinking in all categories, its CEO, under pressure from stockholders, proposed a merger with Hewlett Packard in an attempt to halt its decline (Daniel 2002, 18).

IBM's PC Strategy

Between 1994 and 1998, IBM's continuous-improvement programs had reduced the number of PC models from 3,400 to 150. The number of components was cut from 420 to 200. In addition IBM hired Dell's former head of procurement. He set up a new supplier pipeline where 60 percent of IBM parts can be delivered within 24 hours. Today 31 percent of IBM's PC components are assembled by sales outlets. In addition, IBM has opened a Web sales site. These changes have brought IBM closer to Dell than Compaq costs (Narisetti 1998, B1). In January of 1998, IBM's PC inventories were still high at retail outlets. In an attempt to reduce inventories from 120 down to 20 days, IBM began to cut PC prices dramatically, extending its price war with Compaq to a new level. However, by April 2002 IBM's PC unit losses still continued to mount, with losses of $500 million in 1999 and $1 billion in 2000 and 2001. IBM discontinued manufacturing and store sales of its desktop PCs (Daniel 2002, 18).

Dell's PC Strategy

Dell's high-speed management model between 1999 and 2002 had increased its U.S. PC market shares from 11 to 24 percent and ranked number one in U.S. market shares. Dell's continuous-improvement program had reduced its operating costs to 10 percent of sales while Compaq's costs were 18 percent of sales, with IBM withdrawing from the PC desktop market. Dell's CEO set a target of 40 percent market share by 2005. In addition Dell decided to take its high-speed management model into two new areas: computer storage, where

3Com held top market share, and networking, where Cisco holds top market share. In both areas the market leaders have 50 percent profit margins. Dell believes it can undersell both firms in such a manner as to take away their customers. 3Com and Cisco claim to welcome the competition, but so did IBM and Compaq in the beginning. In 2001 Dell held 13.3 percent of world PC sales, Compaq 11 percent, and IBM 6 percent. Dell plans to expand its 8 percent overseas sales in the next three years to 20 percent. Only time will tell if Dell continues its domination of these markets. However, as Compaq and IBM will testify, Dell is a formidable competitor with its High-Speed Management business model, which is difficult to imitate and hard to beat (Daniel 2002, 18).

Conclusions Regarding the Benchmarking of *Dell Computer* and *High-Speed Management Theory*

The direct [business] model turned out to have several other benefits that even Michael Dell couldn't have anticipated when he founded the company. "You actually get to have a relationship with customers and that creates valuable information, which, in turn, allows us to leverage our relationship with both suppliers and customers. Couple that information with technology, and you have the infrastraucture to revolutionize the fundamental business models of major global companies."

(Margretta 1998: 73–74)

Certainly our benchmarking of the Dell Computer Company's four rapid-response systems provides strong support for our High-Speed Management communication theory. Dell's best practices does support the *first proposition of High-Speed Management, namely that reducing the cycle time an organization takes in getting its products and services to market yields increases in productivity, quality, market shares, profits, management and worker motivation and commitment, and customer satisfaction.* Dell's best practices also provide strong support for *High-Speed management's second proposition, namely that improving an organization's communication is the most significant ingredient for reducing cycle time.* Removing communication bottlenecks, standardizing information transfer, developing rapid-response systems, and improving the quality and adaptation of messages to all organization stakeholders are central to reduced cycle time.

However, our benchmarking of Dell's best practices has revealed several important insights into effective organizational communication processes.

First, Dell's four rapid-response systems are critical success factors for achieving the organization's results because they place all of the organization's stakeholders in real-time interactive communication relationships with each other.

Second, Dell's four profiling activities are necessary backbone communication processes for guiding communication content, so it is precisely adapted to all Dell's stakeholders. The use of profiling and report cards makes sure that the content of interaction is focused on customer needs, product use, customer service issues, and value-chain performance targets. Without these backbone processes, speed of response would lose its focus on improved organizational performance.

Third, benchmarking targets are necessary to reveal what world-class performance is at a given point in time and how it is achieved. However, these targets are transitory; they change as customer needs, competitors' performance, and new implementing processes emerge. To be effective, targets must undergo significant updating to meet the above mentioned changes.

Fourth, a good continuous-improvement program is necessary to rework critical success factors and targets in order to stay ahead of competitors and in touch with stakeholders while improving performance.

Fifth, once again the power of direct and continuous interaction on the Internet with all a firm's stakeholders in real time indicates the appropriate use of technology for implementing interpersonal relationships among a firm's stakeholders and creating a community of interests in a firm's success.

Sixth, while our benchmarking of Dell's best practices provides strong support for High-Speed Management theory, this same research suggests that the theory needs to be modified or expanded. The theory needs to include profiling, report cards, and direct interaction among stakeholders in real time to guide the content of communication and to place communication within an interpersonal relationship. Only then will the results of this inquiry tightly fit the theory's prediction in regard to reducing cycle time through improved communication.

Finally, in May of 1999, fifteen executives of major firms, plus a few consultants and professors, spent a day holed up in the faculty lounge at Harvard University. The purpose of this one-day meeting was to discuss the opportunities and threats posed by the rise of the Internet and e-business. This discussion centered on a benchmarking study of Dell, Compaq, and IBM PC units similar to the one provided above. As the discussion progressed, the participants began using the word "Dell" as a verb. They concluded that the CEOs of Compaq's and IBM's PC units had been fired in part because they had been "Delled," outflanked by low price, high quality products from an Internet integrated and digitized Dell. Ted Rybeck, Chair of Cambridge Consulting and Benchmarking Partners, Inc., and host of the meeting closed by suggesting, "You want to be the Deller rather than the Dellee of your industry" (Wysocki 1999, A1). Dell has thus pioneered the use of High-Speed Management using the Internet and its rapid-response capabilities to dominate the PC industry.

References

Altany, D.C. (1992). Benchmarkers unite. *Industry Week* 24 (February): 1–8.

Barrons, P. and Sager, I. (1989). PC makers think beyond the box. *Business Week*, April 19, 148–150.

Chowdhury, N. (June 21, 1999). Dell cracks China. *Fortune,* June 21, 120-121.

Cullin, R., and Cushman D. (1999). *Managing Governmental Competitiveness: Speed, Consensus, and Performance.* Albany: State University of New York Press.

Cushman, D. and King, S.S. (1995). *Communication and High-Speed Management.* Albany: State University of New York Press.

———. (1997). *High-Speed Management: The Role of Communication in Continuously Improving an Organization's Performance.* Albany: State University of New York Press.

Daniel, C. (2002). Dell seeks new routes for its lean machine. *Financial Times,* April 2, 18.

Dell. (2002). *Dell Fact Sheet.* www.Dell.com.

Dell Computer Corporation (1999).

Dell Home Systems Catalog, May.

Dumaine, B. (1989). How managers can succeed through speed. *Fortune,* February 12, 54–59.

Elstron, P. (1999). Advertisement. *Business Week,* March 22, EB35.

Fraker, S. (1984). High-Speed Management for the high tech age. *Fortune*, March 5, 62–69.

Hamilton, D. (1999). Computer industry's focus shifts to market for servers. *Wall Street Journal*, February 23, B4.

———. (1999). PC shipments rose in period; Compaq slips. *Wall Street Journal*, April 26, A3.

———. (1999). Dell surpasses Compaq in U.S. PC sales. *Wall Street Journal*, October 25, A3.

Hansell, S.C. (1999).Compaq says profit outlook is troubled. *New York Times*, April 10, B1.

Kehoe, L. (1999). Pfeiffer becomes a victim of his own success. *Financial Times*, April 20, 21.

Kirkpatrick, D. (1998). Houston, we have some problems. *Fortune*, June 23, 102–105.

McWilliams G. (1997). Whirlwind on the Web. *Business Week,* April 7.

———. (1999a). Dell Computer to launch workstation with two Intel chips, aggressive pricing. *Wall Street Journal*, March 3, B6.

———. (1999b). Dell Computer to increase sales of cheaper PCs. *Wall Street Journal*, April 9, B2.

———. (1999c). Compaq's stock skids on profit warning. *Wall Street Journal*, April 13, A3.

———. (1999d). Dell's new push: Cheaper laptops built to order. *Wall Street Journal*, July 0, B1.

———. (1999e). Dell fiscal third-quarter profits fell 25%. *Wall Street Journal*, November 22.

———. (1999f). Dell takes aim at home market with Web PC device. *Wall Street Journal*, November 30, B4.

McWiliams, G., and White, J. (1999). Dell to derail: Get into gear online. *Wall Street Journal*, December 1, B1.

Markoff, J. (1999). The PC industry shows strong growth. *New York Times*, October 6, C4.

Margretta, R. (1998). The power of virtual integration: An interview with Dell Computer's Michael Dell. *Harvard Business Review*, March/April, 73-84.

Narisetti, R. (1998). How IBM turned around its ailing PC division. *Wall Street Journal*, March 12, B-1.

Park, A., and Burrows, P. (2001). The conqueror. *Business Week*. September 24, 92–102.

Ramstad, K. E. (1999). Dell builds an electronic super store on the Web. *Wall Street Journal*, March 3, B1.

Rosenbush, S. (1997). Climbing Dell flexes new Internet Service. *USA Today*, July 7, B3.

Schmul, J. (1999). PC legend in the making. *USA Today*, December 6, 1B.

Serwer, A. (1998). Michael Dell rocks. *Fortune*, May 16, 59–70.

———. (2002). Dell does automation. *Fortune*, January 21, 7, 74.

Stepanek, M. (1998). What does Number One do for an encore? *Business Week*, November 2, 51–52.

Versey, J. (1991). The new competitors: They think in terms of speed to market. *Academy of Management Executives*, 2:23–33.

Wysocki, B., Jr. (1999). Corporate caveat: Dell or be Delled. *Wall Street Journal*, May 10, A1.

3

Best Practices at the General Electric Company: Benchmarking a World-Class Leadership Communication System

The two greatest corporate leaders in this country are Alfred Sloan of General Motors and Jack Welch of GE. And Welch would be the greater of the two because he set a new contemporary paradigm for the corporation that is the model for the 21ˢᵗ century.

(Tichy, 1998:93)

In February 2001, General Electric was named Fortune's "Most Admired Company" for the fifth year in a row and named the World's Most Respected Company by the *Financial Times* for the fourth time (Immelt 2001, 1). Jack Welch is the CEO of GE and he is considered one of the world's most successful leaders. In 1999 he was named the most important business leader of the century by *Fortune Magazine,* the most outstanding leader in the world by *Financial World Magazine,* and the Most Respected Business Leader in the World in a survey conducted in the business community by the European newspaper the *Financial Times* (Corrigan 1999, I). GE's performance over the past six years is outlined in table 3.1.

Why have GE and Jack Welch received such accolades? There are at least three reasons.

First, Jack Welch's twenty-year reign as CEO of General Electric has produced rather dramatic results. GE's sales rose from $27.9

Table 3.1
GE's Six-Year Performance Record, 1996–2001
in millions of dollars

	2001	2000	1999	1998	1997	1996
Sales	125,913	129,853	111,630	100,469	90,804	79,179
Profits	13,684	12,735	10,720	9,296	8,203	7,280

Source: *GE Annual Reports,* 1996–2001.

31

billion in 1981 to $129.7 billion in 2000; profits rose from $2.9 billion to $12.7 billion; and market value rose from $12 billion to $500 billion. By 2000 GE had become America's *fifth* largest industrial corporation in sales, the *first* largest in profits, and the *first* largest in stockholder value (Moore and Brady 2000, 130).

Second, GE's competitors are among the largest and most powerful firms in the world. These global electronic and electrical equipment firms include Hitachi, Matsushita Electric, SONY, Toshiba, Mitsubishi Electric, NEC, Siemens, Royal Philips Electric, and ABB. Each year from 1990 to 2000, GE earned $1 billion more in profits than the combined profits of these nine firms. Such a performance suggests that GE has significantly more successful leadership than its industry competitors.

Third, and perhaps most significant, over thirty of GE's former top-level executives have become CEOs of such successful global firms as GTE, Allied Signal, Goodyear Tire, Cal Pine, Fiat, Owens-Corning, Iomega, SPX, Ryland Group, Conseco, General Dynamics, Terra Lyco, 3M, Home Depot, Wang Laboratories, Sundstrand, Great Lakes Chemical, Rubbermaid, M/A Communications, Stanley Works, USF&G, Zorn Industries, Clean Harbor, Pentair, Intuit, Primedia, TRW, and Systems Computer Technology. This suggests that GE's and Jack Welch's leadership system is principled, systemic, and teachable, rather than a function of one man's unique abilities. Therefore, GE's management system warrants careful study by all corporate leaders seeking to improve.

Our benchmarking study of GE's leadership system will proceed in three stages consisting of an examination of (1) the critical success factors and backbone communications processes employed by Jack Welch; (2) the targets and implementing structures employed in achieving these critical success factors and in utilizing the backbone communication processes; and (3) conclusions regarding the benchmarking of this leadership system.

Benchmarking Critical Success Factors

Welch was hardly the first person to see the new world coming. His great achievement is that having seen it, he faced up to the huge, painful changes it demanded, and made them faster and more emphatically than anyone else in the business. He led managers into this new world, which we still inhabit, and just as important, he showed business people everywhere a method of attacking change of any kind.

(Colvin, 1999:186)

In his twenty years as CEO of GE, Jack Welch led his firm through three strategic transformations. These transformations represent the three critical success factors of his leadership system.

First, Jack Welch transformed GE to the most competitive and valuable firm in the world. Here he repositioned his firm into markets and businesses which were high-growth, high-margin, global businesses where GE could become number 1 or 2 in market shares.

Second, he transformed GE into a boundaryless firm through speed, simplicity, and self-confidence. Here he restructured GE's internal management processes, leadership training, communication, and continuous-improvement systems to provide his firm with the ability to constantly change in order to respond to a rapidly changing competitive environment and to stay on top.

Third, he transformed GE into a multipolar, multicultural, global Internet service firm. Here he globalized GE in markets, sourcing, and management through acquisitions, joint ventures, and alliances. This extended GE's reach and dominance to every corner of the globe.

These three transformations are the critical success factors necessary for implementing GE's world-class leadership system. Equally important are the backbone leadership communication processes employed to guarantee the achievement of the critical success factors. Welch correctly perceived the human tendency to oppose change. He therefore developed a message structure which transformed this natural human tendency into a desire or even passion for change. This message structure consists of six stages, with each stage being repeated in each transformation:

1. Anticipation of an environmental threat which requires a major organizational change in order for the firm to achieve a new environmental fit.

2. Creation and articulation of a clear and persuasive vision for guiding the firm's reorientation processes.

3. Creation of a tension within the firm's operating systems sufficient to overcome the natural tendency to not want to change.

4. Constructive release of that tension through new implementing structures which educate and empower point people to lead the change and gain the support of a firm's stakeholders in bringing about the change.

5. Manifestation of productive results from the implementation of the new change which can serve as a model or benchmark for others within the firm.

6. Introduction of a culture of change which creates a realization in a firm's stakeholders that this process must be repeated again and again, and that GE's leadership system can successfully guide such changes.

These then are the critical success factors and backbone communication processes which undergird Jack Welch's leadership style and GE's leadership systems. Attention is now directed to Welch's use of this system in guiding GE's three major transformations, the targets employed, and the implementing structures for achieving successful change.

Benchmarking GE's Targets

The globalization of General Electric may be the greatest legacy of Jack Welch's 19 years as CEO. An incomparable management tool kit and a passion for growing leaders made it possible.

(Stewart, 1999:124)

In this section we shall explore each of Welch's transformations of GE in turn, paying specific attention to the targets employed, implementing structures put in place, and the backbone communication processes utilized.

Transformation #1: To the Most Competitive and Valuable Firm in the World

In 1981 Jack Welch became CEO of the General Electric Corporation and immediately anticipated GE's first threat and thus the need for a transformational change. Welch (1988, 12) recalls his thoughts:

> At the beginning of the decade . . . we faced a world economy that would be characterized by slower growth with stronger global competitors going after a smaller pie. In the context of that environment we had one clear-cut major competitor: Japan, Inc. . . . powerful . . . innovative . . . and moving aggressively into many of our markets.

Goals

In an attempt to create and operationalize a transformational vision, Welch set two clear and simple goals for his firm and outlined several targets for reaching those goals.

1. To become the most competitive corporation in the world.
This goal challenges GE to become the most profitable firm in the
world. The targets for achieving this goal were operationalized to
mean that each of GE's 12 businesses should (a) invest only in products with high growth potential where GE can become number 1 or
2 in market shares in the world; (b) increase productivity, profits, and
quality 15 percent per year; (c) increase inventory turns to 6 per year;
(d) decentralize power and responsibility downward in order to make
each business unit as fast and flexible as possible in responding to
global competition; (e) monitor carefully the ability of each business
to meet its targets; and (f) intervene when necessary to make each
business become a "win-aholic" (Cushman and King 1994).

2. To become the nation's most valuable corporation. This
goal refers to GE becoming the nation's "most valuable" firm in terms
of market capitalization. The targets for meeting this goal were that
GE (a) keep operating profits rising from 10 to 15 percent; (b) keep
stock appreciation and yield at about 10 to 15 percent per year; (c)
shift the earnings mix so 50 percent comes from a high-growth area;
(d) aggressively pursue a stock repurchase program; (e) expand
exports to 50 percent of sales; and (f) maintain management's reputation as an entrepreneurial, agile, knowledgeable, aggressive, and
effective competitor (Cushman and King 1994).

Implementing Structures

Jack Welch created an organizational tension in 1981 aimed at motivating these changes by redefining his firm's goals and targets. He
then released the tension in a series of dramatic and now famous
moves. *First*, he cut GE's 150 independent business units down to 12,
each positioned in a high-growth, high-margin industry in which GE
ranked number 1 or 2 in market shares in the world. *Second*, between 1981 and 1993, Welch sold over 200 of GE's business centers,
worth $12 billion, while acquiring 300 business centers, worth $26
billion. He closed 78 production facilities and invested $25 million in
automating the remaining 200 U.S. facilities and the 130 abroad in 24
countries in order to make them world-class manufacturing facilities. *Third*, Welch shed over 150,000 employees, one out of every
four workers. He reduced 9 layers of management to 5, while releasing one out of every four managers. *Fourth*, he decentralized power,
expanded his managers' span of control, built an all-new executive
team, and restructured every business, replacing 11 of 12 business
leaders *Finally*, the recession in the United State in the early 1980s
allowed GE to acquire firms and employees with high potential by

carefully reviewing the available options and then acquiring those firms at a 50 to 75 percent lower price than normal (Cushman and King 1994).

Welch realized that GE had to undertake framebreaking changes if it was to meet the challenge of becoming a world-class competitive organization. Welch (1988, 2) sketched his vision and described its roots:

> Our experience during the late '70's in grappling with world competition etched very clearly on our minds the belief that companies that held on to marginal businesses—or less than world-competitive operations of *any* sort—wouldn't be around for very long. That analysis led us to a strategy that said we had to be number one or number two in each one of our businesses . . . or we had to see a way to get there . . . or exit if we couldn't. The product businesses had to achieve global leadership positions in cost, quality and technology. Our services businesses had to define and attain leading niche positions in the broad spectrum of markets they served. That was—that is— our strategy: simple, even stark.

In 1988, Welch stood back and reflected on this effort:

> Now, how we went at this can be described from two totally different perspectives. One perspective would use words like "downsizing," "reducing," "cutting." We think that view misses the point. We see our task as a totally different one aimed at liberating, facilitating, unleashing the human energy and initiative of our people.
>
> We found that the leaders—people with a vision and a passion—soon began to stand out. And when they did, we found our own self-confidence growing to the point that we began to delegate authority further and further down into the company. Businesses were allowed to develop their own pay plans and incentives that made sense for *their* marketplaces. They were given the freedom to spend significant sums on plant and equipment on their own, based on *their* needs, *their* judgement, *their* view of their marketplace. Freeing people to move rapidly and without hesitation makes all the difference in the world. . . . [W]e have found what we believe is the distilled essence of competitiveness—the reservoir of talent and creativity and energy that can be found in each of our people. That essence is liberated when we make people believe that what they think and do is important . . . and then get out of their way while they do it.

Transformation #2: To a Boundaryless Firm
Through Speed, Simplicity, and Self-Confidence

In April of 1988 this first massive reengineering effort was all but complete and Welch began to anticipate a new threat and thus the need for a second transformation in GE. Welch (1988, 4) reflected,

> [T]oday the world is even tougher and more crowded. Korea and Taiwan have become world-class competitors, as hungry and aggressive as Japan was in 1981. Europe is on fire with a new entrepreneurial spirit and leadership that is among the world's best. Many of its most aggressive companies, like Electrolux and ASEA of Sweden, Philips of Holland, and Siemens and Bayer of Germany, are after our markets through acquisitions and joint ventures—just as we are going after theirs. At the same time, the Japanese are more sophisticated and aggressive than ever—building servicing plants outside Japan, including dozens just over the Mexican border.

By 1988, GE's threats were both external and internal and even larger than in 1981. Welch (1988, 1–2) reflects, "We had to find a way to combine the power, resources, and reach of a *big* company with the hunger, the agility, the spirit, and the fire of a *small* company." The rationale for this change was simple: only the most productive, high quality, and rapid-response firms were going to win in the 1990s. If a top-quality product could not be produced at the world's lowest price and put on the market in less time than competitors, that firm was going to be out of the game. In such an environment, a 15 percent increase in productivity, profits, and quality would not be enough; more would be needed.

Welch then raised the performance targets in regard to his previous goals of becoming the most competitive and valuable corporation in the world. This included increasing productivity and quality from targets of 15 to 20 percent per year, increasing inventory turns from 6 to 10 per year, and increasing stock appreciation from 15 to 20 percent per year.

Goals

The transformation Welch envisioned was a move to a boundaryless firm. In GE's annual report in 1988 Welch outlined this vision as one in which "we knock down the walls that separate us from each other on the inside and from our key constituencies on the outside." The boundaryless company, he said, will remove barriers between functions, levels, and locations. It will reach out to key suppliers and stakeholders to make them part of a single process in which "they and we join hands and intellects in a common purpose—satisfying customers." Welch then called for GE to reorient its corporate vision to "speed, simplicity and self-confidence." Only through boundarylessness, Welch argued, could the corporation reach its initial goals of being the most competitive and valuable firm in the world. In order to operationalize this vision, two new goals and sets of targets were put in place:

   3. To develop open communication based on speed, candor and trust. This goal was operationalized to mean sharing with all employees the corporation's vision, goals, targets, and values, and opening each employee up to discussion regarding the company's and the employee's strengths, weaknesses, and possibility for change. This was accomplished by speaking openly and listening carefully to discussions aimed at preparing, articulating, refining, and gaining acceptance for unit visions; showing candor and trust in sharing and evaluating business and personal plans and performance data; and motivating employees to become more open, more self-confident, more energized individuals in generating and employing practical and technical knowledge (Cushman and King 1994).

   4. To develop a skilled, self-actualizing, productive, and aggressive workforce capable of generating and employing practical and technical innovations. This goal was operationalized to mean that GE wants to create an environment that is a challenging place to work and that will significantly enhance worker skills so that they can find another job if the company no longer needs them— a place where employees are ready to go but eager to stay. In order to actualize this goal GE must (a) develop employee awareness that the only road to job security is increasing market shares and profits; (b) develop employees who are more action oriented, risk oriented, and people oriented; (c) develop employees who relentlessly pursue individual and group goals; (d) develop employee skills and performance through timely and quality education programs; (e) hold employees responsible for meeting productivity and financial targets; and (f) reward high performance and deal effectively with low performance (Cushman and King 1994).

Implementing Structures

Three new mechanisms were put forward to create and release the tension necessary for achieving these new goals: a world-class leadership development program; a world-class continuous improvement program, and a world-class rapid response communication system.

GE's Leadership Development Program. Creating a world-class leadership development program was accomplished through clear criteria for recruiting high potential leaders, socializing them into a new leadership value system, subjecting them to intensive skill and judgement development in action training programs, and then monitoring and rewarding them in such a manner as to develop speed, simplicity, and self-confidence.

GE's leadership development program begins with recruiting. The company does not recruit straight-A students from the world's top MBA programs. Instead GE wants potential leaders with a B+ average from a variety of majors who worked their way through college and who were on a successful sports team or perhaps ran some club. GE hires about 2,000 professionals a year (Murray 1999, 1B)

Next, high potential leaders are socialized into GE's management value system:

G.E. Management Values

G.E. leaders, always with unyielding integrity:

*

Create a clear, simple, reality-based, customer-focused vision and are able to communicate it straightforwardly to all constituencies.

*

Set aggressive targets, understanding accountability and commitment, and are decisive.

*

Have a passion for excellence, hating bureaucracy and all the nonsense that comes with it.

*

Have the self-confidence to empower others and behave in a boundaryless fashion. They believe in and are committed to "Work-Out" as a means of empowerment and are open to ideas from anywhere.

*

Have, or have the capacity to develop, global brains and global sensitivity and are comfortable building diverse global teams.

*

Stimulate and relish change and are not frightened or paralyzed by it, seeing change as opportunity, not threat.

*

Have enormous energy and ability to energize and invigorate others. They understand speed as a competitive advantage and see the total organizational benefits that can be derived from a focus on speed.

(Tichy and Charon 1989, 119)

In 1992 Jack Welch outlined the role which GE's management values system plays in the development of a leader. Welch argued that there are two dimensions to leadership: following through on commitments and doing so employing GE's management value system. He then described four types of leaders at GE and how they are to be treated by the firm.

The first type of leader lives up to commitments and adheres to GE values, empowering and energizing company employees, focusing on the customer, resisting bureaucracy, cutting across boundaries, and thinking globally. This type of person is a prototypical GE leader, one whose skills are renowned among American campuses and headhunters.

The second type of leader does not meet commitments and does not share values. GE gets rid of such leaders quickly.

The third type of leader fails to fulfill commitments but shares GE's values. He or she deserves a second chance following training, preferably in a different environment. The final type of leader is the old type, who delivers on commitments but does not share GE's values. Welch (1992) argues,

> And perhaps this type was more acceptable in easier times; but in an environment where we must have every good idea from every man and woman in the organization, we cannot afford management styles that suppress and intimidate. Whether we can convince and help these managers to change—recognizing how difficult that can be—or part company with them if they cannot, will be the ultimate test of our commitment to the transformation of this company and will determine the future of the mutual trust and respect we are building. (Hyatt and Naj 1992, B1).

While being socialized into GE's management value system, high potential leaders are subjected to GE's intensive leadership training programs. During their first two years with GE, the new recruits are placed in functional corporate training programs. For example, engineers would be involved in three eight-month action projects dealing with actual problems to be solved at GE and they would be expected to solve them. Interwoven into these three projects would be classroom work in project management, process improvement, and Six-Sigma quality. These projects and class work require 10 to 20 hours of homework each week. Similar courses are taught in marketing, manufacturing, finance, sales, and so forth. At the same time, recruits are assigned to and rotated through jobs across businesses two or three times in two years.

Next, GE selects the top 50 to 100 performers from the first two-year training programs to put on GE's audit staff. This is considered fast-tracking at GE. GE, unlike most firms, does not consider its audit staff as an accounting unit. It uses its staff as a further training ground for young leaders. During the two-year stint, these leaders swarm across the company's many business units, spending the first year checking their books and the second acting as outside consultants on performance improvements. This opportunity to visit, check, and advise multipolar business units around the world is invaluable in providing a global perspective on GE (Murray 1999, B14).

Finally, after two years on the audit staff, these high-potential leaders are assigned to positions and projects throughout GE's businesses. They are rotated to other jobs in other units every two years. "The real training is the day-to-day job and being given a job substantially more difficult than you or anyone else thinks you're ready for," says GE veteran Tom Tiller, who is now CEO of a non-GE firm (Murray 1999, B14).

GE's top 300 leaders are reviewed by its board of directors and Jack Welch once a year. The company's top 3,000 leaders are reviewed by Welch once a year. These evaluations are based primarily on four criteria: (1) meeting and exceeding performance targets, (2) 360-degree reviews from all GE stakeholders, (3) the sharing of best practices with other units, and (4) the development of the leadership talent of subordinates. Each GE leader is ranked 1 through 5 on this performance based on the above data. A number 1 ranking can be given only to the top 10 percent of leaders, number 2 to the next 15 percent, number 3 to the middle 50 percent, number 4 to the next 15 percent, who are considered marginal leaders, and number 5 to the bottom 10 percent who are to be let go.

At GE, exceptional performance is rewarded by stock options, bonuses, and promotions. All number 1 ranked leaders are given both stock options and bonuses. Ninety percent of number 2 ranked leaders are given smaller valued stock options and bonuses, with 10 percent given one but not the other. Fifty percent of number 3 ranked leaders are given stock options, the others fifty percent bonuses. In 1998, 1,200 of GE's leaders had received stock options through the years that had made them millionaires, and that involved 800 leaders below the level of senior management. GE's bonuses can range between 25 and 150 percent of base pay. Each of GE's leaders are reviewed in verbal and written form in what is termed a "C session." In this meeting a leader's strengths and weaknesses are assessed as the leader commits to an improvement agenda with fixed targets. After the interview, a letter is sent repeating the agenda committed to and the targets and this document becomes a basis for evaluation in the next round of assessment (Stewart 1999, 136; Byrne 1998, 102).

GE's Continuous-Improvement Program. By late 1988, Welch noticed that most of his top management team and business leaders had bought into GE's transformation, but middle and line managers were still prone to fight or ignore the need to change. The mechanism put in place to alter these behaviors was a new continuous-improvement program called "Workout." Workout was designed to ensure that employees, suppliers, and customers could suggest needed changes candidly to managers without fear of retribution, thus placing pressure to change on middle and line managers from above and below. As Welch had hoped, the process quickly exposed GE managers who did not "walk the talk."

Workout was a world-class continuous-improvement program which included (1) a self-managed teamwork program called a "New England Town Meeting," (2) a cross-functional teamwork program called "process mapping," (3) a benchmarking or "best practices" teamwork program, and (4) an aggressive outside linking/joint ventures teamwork program (King and Cushman 1994). The practical objective of workout was to "get rid of thousands of bad habits accumulated since the creation of GE 112 years ago. The intellectual goal was to put the leaders of each business in front of 100 or so employees, eight to ten times a year to let them know what their people think about how the company can be improved and then make the leaders respond to those changes. Ultimately we are restructuring the leader-subordinate relationship to challenge both to make GE a better place to work. It will force leaders and workers to combine in creating a vision, articulating the vision, passionately owning the vision, and relentlessly driving it to completion" (Tichy and Charon 1989, 113).

By the end of 1997, over 200,000 employees participated in three-day New England Town Meetings with remarkable results. In GE's plastic division alone, over thirty workout teams have been empowered to make changes. One team saved GE plastics $2 million by modifying one production process, another enhanced productivity four-fold, while a third reduced product delivery time 400 percent (*Workout* 1991, 1–2). Another business, NBC, used Workout to halt the use of report forms that totaled more than two million pieces of paper a year (Stewart 1991, 44). GE Credit Services used Workout to tie its cash registers directly to the mainframe, cutting the time for opening a new account from 30 minutes to 90 seconds. Similar results have been reported from Workout projects in each of GE's other businesses, demonstrating a remarkable company-wide reorientation of coalignment processes among customers, suppliers, and worker capabilities and organizational needs.

As GE's top management team reviewed the projects which had been successful from their Workout programs they noticed a difference in the types of programs which had saved a million dollars from those which saved 100 million. The latter always involved changes in organizational processes which spanned the entire value chain. They cut across departments and involved linking with suppliers and customers. All emphasized managing processes, not functions. This led GE to establish its cross-functional teamwork program aimed at mapping and then improving key organizational processes. Such process maps frequently allowed employees to see and understand organizational processes from beginning to end for the first time. They also demonstrated the need for a new type of manager, a process manager who could coalign an organization's total assets. The process maps allowed employees to spot bottlenecks, time binds, inventory shortages, and overflows. Since implementing such a process mapping teamwork program, GE has cut its 16-week appliance manufacturing cycle in half, while increasing product availability 6 percent and decreasing inventory costs 20 percent. The program has cost less than $3 million to implement and has already returned profits 100 times that (Stewart 1991, 48).

While this internal transformation of GE's value chain was taking place, Jack Welch also realized that some other global organizations were achieving greater productivity, profits, quality, flexibility, adaptability, and rapid-response time than GE. In the summer of 1988, GE began its Best Practices Program aimed at locating those organizations which had out performed GE in a given area, developing a case study of how they did it, and then employing these case studies as world-class benchmarks for improving GE's performance. GE scanned the globe and located twenty-four corporations which had outperformed GE in some area. It then screened out direct competitors and companies which would not be credible to GE employees. Welch then invited each corporation to come to GE to learn about its best practices in return for allowing GE to come to those companies and study their best practices. About one-half of the companies agreed. They included AMP, Chapparral Steel, Ford, Hewlett Packard, Xerox, and three Japanese companies. GE sent out observers to develop case studies and ask questions. These best practices case studies have been turned into a course at Crotonville, GE's leadership training center that is offered to a new class of managers from each of GE's 12 businesses each month (Stewart 1991, 44–45).

GE's Rapid-Response System. The third mechanism GE put in place to create and release tension necessary to achieve goals was a rapid-response communication system. This system functioned at four levels. The first level was a *Quick Market Intelligence System* designed to link customers with GE. This system was designed to dramatically speed up information flow to and from the market. Monday through Thursday, issues were generated by sales force employees regarding growth opportunities, competitor moves, quality problems, and process delivery issues and sent to Friday's business meeting. This meeting would include business leaders and about 60 to 70 unit leaders. They would explore and act on each issue raised. Friday afternoon, this meeting's decisions were sent by interactive TV directly to regions and plants where they were discussed in a teleconference with the people raising the issues to see if the solutions were workable. If not, the decision makers changed their decision. This rapid turnaround-time, customer-focused decision making energizes change and overcomes resistance to change, while involving customers, management, and workers equally in the action plan. While it used to take 14 weeks to get an order, make the product, and then sell it, in some businesses GE has cut that time to days, saving billions of dollars in costs each year (Donion 1993, 6).

The second level involves the *interactions between workers and managers in Workout sessions,* which are taped to make sure every useful suggestion by employees is quickly and decisively responded to by management with appropriate action and resource levels. These tapes are reviewed by one of Jack Welch's aides and where appropriate action was not taken, the manager's decision is reviewed and corrected within days of the meeting. GE finds about 90 percent of its ideas for improvement from workers at such workout meetings (Donion 1993, 6).

The third level involves a once a year conference in which each business, organizational process, and functional unit is invited to present important cost-saving practices developed in the past year. This conference involves the top 800 managers at GE and serves as a rapid-diffusion device for spreading new innovations developed within GE's twelve businesses (Cushman and King 1995). Jack Welch (1993, 1) put it this way:

> What is unique about G.E. is that each business is autonomous in its marketplace. And each is a big company in itself: $7 billion in aircraft engines, $6 billion in power systems, $5 billion in plastics. But each ends up being a laboratory for us, as each has an idea or initiative and each sets the bar higher to achieve. We can take the idea of one and move then to the next, and the next and the next. So the job at the top of this company is to take the wonderful initiatives found in multiple businesses and add to them or, with the speed of light, transfer them to other businesses. (Welch 1993b:1)

This once-a-year meeting is supplemented by cross-business councils in the various organizational functions aimed, according to Welch, "at moving intellectual capital—taking ideas and moving them around faster and faster." There is a marketing council, HR council, sales council, manufacturing council, quality council, and so forth. Each business operates similar cross-business and cross-functional councils which meet for a day or two every few months and operate online daily. Every leader sits on at least one of these cross business councils. At meetings, every member is expected to bring and share new ideas to improve performance (Stewart 1999, 132).

The fourth level is the *Corporate Executive Council* meetings held for two days each quarter, including all 12 business leaders and their staff members. Here top management reviews, coordinates, and resources individual units' plans and strategies while sharing corporate intelligence. At these meetings, business plans and implementing strategies are subject to the scrutiny of top management and the other 11 business leaders for critique and suggestions for improvement. These sessions are frequently very heated and participants have termed such meetings "open kimono time" to symbolize how poorly designed plans and strategies and the advocates can be subjected to exposure.

These four levels of communication systems provide rapid and responsive decisions and information diffusion, which allows GE to function with speed, simplicity, and self-assurance.

Perhaps the most important measure of the effectiveness of GE's new leadership development, continuous-improvement, and rapid-communications systems can be observed in GE's head-to-head competition with its chief competitors in the global electrotechnology industry. As early as 1990, GE led the industry competitors in sales per employee, return on sales, growth in revenues, market value growth, value added growth, profit margins, and before tax profits (Harnischfeger, von der Weans, and Haven 1993, 23).

A recession in Europe in the mid-1990s allowed GE to acquire firms and employees with unusually high potential at costs 50 to 70 percent lower than in nonrecession times. Between 1990 and 1999, GE's European operations grew from "10 to 35 billion in sales," (Stewart 1999, 124, 136). GE could thus increase its excellence and reduce its costs both at the same time.

Between 1988 and 1994 Welch watched with pride as GE's sales grew 15 to 20 percent per year, operating margins rose from 10 to 15 percent, and inventory turns increased from 6 to 10 per year. However, several serious problems also began to emerge. GE's locomotive unit experienced problems with motors shorting out in railcars provided to the Montreal Transit System, leaving 8,000 commuters stranded and shutting the line down for 19 days while the problem was fixed. GE's turbine unit, which provided gas turbines for power plants around the world, discovered cracks in the turbines. The cost of fixing this flaw ran to $200 million. GE's jet engine unit failed an FDA test for its new engine, which was developed to power Boeing's 777 aircraft, delaying the planes' delivery to customers by six weeks to one year (Carley 1999, A1). Such problems as these according to Welch were costing GE $8 to $12 billion a year while eroding customer confidence in GE's products (Byrne 1998, 98).

Welch responded to these problems quickly and decisively in 1995 by undertaking a new quality control program modeled on Motorola's highly successful Six Sigma Program. This program allows managers to set clear performance measures and track and reward employee improvements. Workout allowed employees to pressure managers to respond. Six Sigma allows managers to pressure employees to respond. In 1995, GE, employing its leadership training and continuous-improvement programs, undertook 200 quality projects, in 1996 3,000 projects, and in 1997 6,000 projects aimed at reducing defects to 3.4 per one million operations. This program was expected to cost GE over $1 billion while saving $7 to $10 billion over the next ten years. Participation in this program was motivated by committing 40 percent of GE's annual bonus system between 1995 and 1997 and 100 percent of its promotion system to having successfully led one or more of these projects. By 1998 over 110,000

GE employees had participated in Six Sigma training programs and projects (Byrne 1998, 98).

The 1990s according to Jack Welch (1988, 4) would be a "white-knuckle decade for global business . . . fast . . . exhilarating" with many winners and losers. But according to Welch GE was ready. His two transformational visions, mobilizations, and institutionalizations in the 1980s had put GE in position to meet these new threats head on with the speed, flexibility, and efficiency of a small creative firm while employing the resources and talent of a large firm. Welch (1988, 4) argues,

> We approach the '90's with a business system, a method of operating, that allows us to routinely position each business for the short- and long-term so that while one or more are weathering difficult markets, the totality is always growing faster than the world economy.
>
> To go with our business strategy, we've got a management system now in place and functioning that supports that strategy—one that is lean, liberating, fast-moving—an organization that facilitates and frees and, above all, understands that the fountainhead of success is the individual, not the system.

Transformation #3: To a Multipolar/Multicultural, Global Internet Service Firm

Between 1981 and 1997 GE had worked hard to increase sales from $27 to $90 billion, profits from $2.9 to $8.2 billion, and stockholder value from $12 to $280 billion. By 1998 GE's various divisions had

Table 3.2
General Electric's Annual Operating Margins
(percentages)

	1996	1997	1998
Information Services	23	23	23
Materials	23	23	23
G.E. Capital	20	20	20
Aircraft Engines	19	18	17
Broadcasting	18	21	22
Medical Systems	17	18	18
Industrial	16	16	17
Power Generation	15	16	26
Appliances	12	12	12

Source: General Electric, "Financial Analysis" (www.GE.com, 1999)

raised operational profit margins to an average of 17 percent across businesses (see table 3.2).

By 1997, the chief threat to GE's continued progress was the high level of performance GE had already achieved. For GE to continue its upward trend in sales, profits, quality, and stockholder value, Jack Welch believed he had to undertake two new courses of action. *First,* he had to raise the general performance levels for GE's management team. Targets for operating margins were raised from 20 to 25 percent, quality control to Six Sigma's, and inventory turns to 12 per year. This in turn required that he raise expectations regarding what types of leaders could meet these new performance expectations:

> We must raise, again, the bar of quality as it applies to ourselves. The reality is we simply can't afford to field anything but teams of "A" players. At the leadership level, an "A" is a man or women who has a vision and the ability to articulate that vision . . . has enormous personal energy and ability to energize others, has an edge, the instinct and courage to make tough decisions. In engineering, "A's" relish the rapid change and continuously reeducate themselves. In manufacturing, "A" players consider inventory an embarrassment. . . . In sales "A" players use the enormous customer value that six sigma & quality program generates to differentiate GE from the competition, to find new accounts and expand old ones. (J. Welch, quoted in Henry 1998, 8B)

Second, GE had to begin its third transformation in 17 years to a multipolar/multicultural Internet firm with a focus on pushing deeper into the high-margin service areas in each GE business (Smart 1996, 155–160; Murray 1999, B1). This globalization process, according to Welch, was to proceed in three stages. First was the globalization of *markets,* acquiring the assets to sell in any market chosen by any business. Second was the globalization of *sources,* being able to buy or build wherever it would be most advantageous. Third was the globalization of *intellect,* going wherever the best leaders were. "It means using Russian engineering and Indian software—not to arbitrage labor costs, but because these are the best people you can find," said Welch (Stewart 1999, 136). In order to obtain the needed increase in operating profit margins, GE's globalization process needed to take advantage of what Jack Welch termed "the greatest change in business in his lifetime, the Internet and e-commerce" (Murray 1999, B1). Thus, this third transformation involved the setting of three new goals and putting in place three new implementing structures.

Goals

5. *GE must become a multipolar, multicultural firm.* This goal
was operationalized to mean that GE's 12 businesses which were
currently number one or two in the world must now become number one or two in the three major markets of the world—the Americas, Europe (including Eastern Europe and the former Soviet Union),
and the Pacific Rim (Japan, China, India, and Southeast Asia). New
targets were set: by the year 2000 one-third of GE's sales and profits
should originate from each of these three markets. In order to meet
these targets, GE had to (a) make acquisitions and form joint ventures and alliances in these new markets; (b) develop profit centers
in each of these markets; (c) develop a multicultural pool of business leaders and employees; and (d) integrate these new acquisitions into their R&D, manufacturing, sales, and service systems. GE's
plan was to employ it's strong infrastructure in technology transfer,
management training, and financial services to broadly and deeply
penetrate these markets.

   **6. *To transform GE into a global Internet company in
which every division is run as an e-business.*** GE in 1998 had 5
percent of its business transactions online. Welch set a target of
increasing this to 50 percent by 2000 and completing the transformation by 2002 (Murray 1999, B1). To assist in the push to meet
these targets, GE had to (a) provide a senior executive for each
business to lead the transformation; (b) set up project teams in
the leadership training and continuous-improvement programs to
focus the firm's efforts; (c) create a "destroyyourbusiness.com"
team in each business to analyze potential Web-based business
models for the unit; (d) create a team of Web fanatics in each
business to move existing business online; (e) make 40 percent of
all bonuses and 100 percent of all promotions tied to this effort; (f)
place all these Internet efforts under the coordination of Gary M.
Reiner, a senior vice president and chief information officer for GE;
and (g) install computer kiosks on factory floors for use by labor-
ers (Murray 1999, B1).

   7. *To expand GE's service function in all its businesses.*
Here Welch set a target of having 50 percent of all sales in each
business come from service by 2000 (Smart 1996, 155–160). This
was to be accomplished by (a) appointing Paola Fresco, a vice president from corporate headquarters, to head the effort, (b) asking
each business to appoint a senior executive to head the process, (c)
making bonuses and promotions tied to this effort, and (d) setting

up leadership training and continuous improvement projects in this area (Smart 1996, 155–160).

Implementing Structures

To meet these three new goals and their targets, three implementing structures were put in place: an acquisition strategy called "smart bombing," an extension of GE's world-class training facilities and financial services into each region of the globe, and the use of GE's leadership training programs and continuous-improvement programs to launch e-commerce activities.

GE's Smart Bombing Linking Strategy. In developing joint ventures, acquisitions, and contracts, GE's divisions can only link with firms where evidence can be provided that such linkages can yield 20 to 25 percent operating profit margins. Prior to any acquisition, joint venture, or alliance, GE sends in a due diligence team to assess the appropriateness of the move. This team normally contains three people: a financial officer to access the books; a transition officer to examine the potential blockers, leaders, and continuous-improvement processes that could be made from inventory reductions to automated manufacturing; and a general manager who will run the operation. From GE's point of view, there are no linking arrangements of equals. GE controls or there is no link. This data is assembled to make the case for acquisition and for linking (Grant 1997, 190).

On the day after an acquisition, a financial officer arrives and the acquired firm goes on GE's accounting system. An integrating manager arrives, normally a new recruit is assigned to lead the integration. A general manager arrives to run the firm and is responsible for profits and losses from day one. This general manager also has targets in regard to sales and profits. Profit margins are expected to be 5 to 10 percent for year two and so on. The integration manager has a 100-day plan which involves getting rid of the blockers and rewarding and sending off for training the high-potential leaders to prevent them from leaving. This usually is worth 2 to 8 percentage points in operating profit margins. Next, the transition manager begins the continuous-improvement initiative aimed at cutting inventory turns, increasing sales, automating manufacturing, and so forth. These changes are usually worth 2 to 8 percent in operating margins. At the end of 100 days, the acquisition, joint venture, or linking process is complete. In 1998 GM made 100 acquisitions worldwide. In 1999, the company made 81 acquisitions or investments in other firms, amounting to $18 billion. This was the largest number of investments of any U.S. firm (Deogun and Scannell 2000, C1)

Developing a World Class Internet Capability. In transforming GE into an Internet firm, Welch set aside resources to assist in the acquisition of world-class Internet companies and personnel. Each of the 12 businesses was asked to put a specific percentage of its investments into this effort. The percent varied from business to business because some, like plastics and GE Capital, were already online (Murray 1999 B1).

Extending GE's World Class Resources into These New Markets. In expanding into these markets, Welch directed GE to (a) develop joint ventures in technology transfer with firms in the region; (b) train foreign nationals in the U.S. and then send them back to Asia and Europe to head GE units; (c) export GE's training programs to the region; and (d) use GE financial services to fund projects in the regions which use GE products (Smart, Engardio, and Smith, 1993). Here Welch sets aside specific amounts of corporate money and personnel to support these efforts. The 12 businesses also use funds and personnel for this purpose.

The expansion into the Pacific Rim, thus far, has generated promising results. GE's-reality based action training programs have taken managers from Asian cultures and trained them in management skills in the U.S. Next these managers were shipped off to the Pacific Rim's major markets to interview old, new, and potential GE customers, competitors, and business managers. Finally, GE asked these managers to develop market-penetration plans and a value chain, reengineering plans to better position the firm's business in the region. Similarly, GE's middle-management training programs are rotating promising multicultural leaders through different businesses and markets in Asia in order to create truly global multipolar, multicultural leaders (Smart, Engardio, and Smith 1993).

GE has invested over $100 million in factories to produce medical imaging equipment, plastics, appliances, and lamps in India. GE sales in India will go from $400 million to $1 billion by the year 2000. The company has moved boldly into China, where the government plans to add $100 billion in power generators, 100 jet engines, 1000 medical imagers, and over 200 locomotives in the next four years. GE Capital has been creative in helping the Chinese government set up a new development bank to fund these activities. In Indonesia GE is part of a $2 billion power plant project and offered an array of technology transfer projects to help upgrade Indonesia's industrial capacities (Smart, Engardio, and Smith 1993). In Malaysia, GE now owns a 49 percent interest in UMW Corporation. In Mexico, GE has over 20 factories with 21,000 employees who have upheld GE appliances as a household name. GE Broadcasting has joined with Rupert Murdoch's Star TV system to launch a new business and news channel throughout the Asian region. Finally GE Capital, a $155 billion per year financial arm, has made $200 million in funds available for loans to small businesses in Asia. In short, GE has been transforming its firm, people, and resources to fit the needs of customers in the Pacific Rim (Stewart, November 8, 1993, 64–70).

By the summer of 1998, Asia's economies were in financial crisis. Malaysia and Hong Kong halted economic growth. In Indonesia, Thailand, and Korea, economic disintegration had set in. Welch set aside $40 billion for GE to begin its bargain hunting in Asia. The acquisition of new firms and talented employees began anew at bargain prices (Murray 1998, B4). Between 1998 and 1999, GE acquired five Japanese firms worth $15.6 billion in sales to add to its five acquisitions worth $4 billion made between 1993 and 1997 (Sapsford 1999, A3). GE's presence in Asia was expected to yield $25 billion in sales in 1999 (Wu Dunn 1994, C1). "The path to greatness in Asia is irreversible and GE will be there," said Welch (Henry 1998, 8B).

GE's expansion into Europe has also yielded promising results. GE Capital is the centerpiece of GE's European strategy. GE's fast growing financial services division has invested over $5 billion in Western and Eastern Europe since 1989. In 1995, according to Koenig, "it looked at roughly 100 deals, bid on 40, and closed on 21" (1996, 17). Major acquisitions were made in Germany, France, Britain, Italy, Poland, Hungary, and Czechoslovakia. In both Eastern and Western Europe, GE Capital has acquired firms with large margins and significant positions in their national markets (Smart, Templeton, and Dwyer 1995, 62).

GE Plastics, Aircraft Engines, medical supplies, and power systems have also expanded their operations in Europe. The lead performer was the GE Plastics division which generated $2 billion in sales in 1995. Its Bergen-op Zoom, Netherlands, plant generates plastics for use in TVs, automobile parts, and other high-value-added products. GE Plastics will soon open a new $500 million silicone plant in Bergen-op-Zoom (Koenig 1996, 118).

GE's European Aircraft Engine Division has a fifty-fifty joint venture with CFMI, a state-owned French aircraft engineer manufacturer Sneeona, which had $2 billion in sales last year. On the strength of their best selling engine, CFMI and GE control 52 percent of the global engine market. In March, 1996 GE Aircraft Engines Europe signed a $2.3 billion ten-year contract to overhaul British Airways engines (Koenig 1996, 118).

GE Europe's Medical Systems posted sales of $1 billion. Its units were consolidating assembly plants using skilled laborers outside of Paris while components were made in low-cost countries like Portugal and Spain (Koenig 1996, 118). In 1999, this unit acquired OLC Medical Systems and Mecon Inc., a software firm (Murray 1999, B4).

GE Europe's Power Systems division in 1994 acquired an Italian turbine manufacturer, Nuove Pignone; in 1998 Alstrom's large turbines; and in 1999 the Anglo-Norwegian firm Kvaener. In 1995, GE's Europe Power System division had sales of $1.2 billion with a noteworthy profit of $300 million. Nuove Pignone recently signed a $1.6 billion contract with RAP Gazprom to replace and modify gas turbines on Russia's pipelines (Koenig 1996, 118).

Finally, not all that GE has touched in Europe turned to gold. GE's Tungsram lighting plant in Hungary had serious financial trouble for over three years, causing GE major losses. It finally edged into the black in 1996 with $500 million in sales. Tungsram is number three in market shares behind Philips and Siemans with an 18 percent share (Koenig 1996, 118). GE's NBC division purchased a second-tier satellite broadcaster called Super Channel as an entry way into Europe. But this firm is losing money and it is unclear when its fate will turn.

GE is no longer an American firm. Its expanded presence in Europe is projected to yield $35 billion in sales in 1999. Its expansion presence in the Pacific Rim is expected to yield $35 billion in sales in 1999. Jack Welch's attempt to become a multipolar, multicultural firm, while not complete, is well on its way to becoming a very profitable reality.

GE's move to become a global Internet firm is also well underway. "The Internet is now part of a leader's necessary skill base," says Gary Reiner, a senior vice president at GE and the officer overseeing GE's Internet push (Murray 1999, B5). At corporate headquarters, GE aggregates its 12 businesses' common supply base and purchases $35 billion of materials and services over the Internet, saving approximately $3 billion per year ("Case Study," 1998, 20).

GE Capital has 24 businesses and they are all online. The division is seeking a software firm for acquisitions to help improve operating profit margins. GE manages credit cards for over 300 firms and in December 1999 announced that all those firms' customers could be billed and pay off their cards online (Sapsford 1999, A4). GE Capital has invested in Internet firms since 1998 to the tune of $8.55 million. Today those holdings are valued at $4.3 billion (Rao 2000, 14). GE plastics is also primarily an online firm. It places electronic sensors in the sites of customers' storage facilities which let the firm know when a new supply is needed. Polymerland, which distributes plastics and other materials to over 3,000 customers, has had an Internet site since 1997 for e-commerce. Here customers can place and track orders, access industry information, pick up technical tips, and post advice to others on a bulletin board (Murray 1999, B4). Sales at Polymerland's e-commerce site have risen from $10,000 per week to $6 million per week in 2000 (Rao 2000, 146).

GE NBC is also an online firm which is rapidly expanding its Internet presence. It runs NBC, MSNBC, and CNBC. More recently NBC has purchased a Net portal, an auto sales unit, a shopping network, an online mall, and an online video provider. CNBC has acquired an online stock firm (Siklos and Brady 1999, 42; Pope 1999, B8; Murray 1999, B4). NBC most recently became a major stockholder in a broadband Internet firm in order to offer high-speed Internet transmissions (Flint 1999, B9).

GE Medical Systems has an Internet monitoring system for service, repair, and supplies of its imaging equipment. This imaging system has been expanded to locomotives, jet engines, power systems, and so forth (Rao 2000, 146). GE Medical has just acquired Mecon Inc., a search engine for medical equipment supplies and costs which provides a database on hospital performance and so on. (Murray 1999, B4). In short GE's 12 businesses have to become Internet and e-commerce businesses by the year 2000.

The expansion of GE's service function to 50 percent of each business over the next five years was well underway by 1996. GE's vice chair Paolo Fresco began this effort by asking each division to appoint a high-level manager responsible to the division CEO to head this effort. He then established a service council which was to meet regularly for these top managers to share ideas on how to expand the service sector of their divisions. By 1996, one year after the initiative began, significant results were already beginning to occur.

GE's Locomotive division has sold 150 DC-powered engines to the Burlington Northern Railroad and signed a contract to service those engines. The service unit has also developed an electronic tracking system to help railroads manage rolling stock. *GE Jet Engines* has signed contracts with British Airways for $2.3 billion to service 80 percent of their engines and with US Airways for $1 billion to service their fleet. *GE Power Systems* has developed major repair and refurbishing facilities in the United States and Europe and predicts that 50 percent of its income will come from this area. It already has in hand $1 billion in contracts for operating and maintaining power plants. *GE Medical Systems* has signed a contract with Columbia/HCA Health Care, which operates 30 hospitals, to maintain and manage their imaging system. The contract has already saved Columbia $10 million dollars. They have contracted with GE to streamline their procurement and management systems. *GE Capital* has spent $5 billion developing computer consulting centers in the United States, Canada, and Europe to help firms develop their own intranets and to effectively utilize computer systems. It has signed a contract with Anderson Consulting to provide technical services for their consulting in their own and other firms (Smart 1996, 155–160).

Our benchmarking case study of GE's leadership system is now complete. We have explored in some detail the critical success factors, backbone communication processes, targets, and implementing structures in order to provide insight into and an understanding of how this firm developed over 30 successful CEOs of Fortune 500 firms. We are now in a position to draw some conclusions regarding GE's best practices in leadership.

Conclusions

The companies that find a way to engage every mind—harvest
every volt of passionate energy—bring excitement to the lives
of their people—and break every artificial barrier between
people—will be the companies that win in the 90s and beyond
and we intend to be the best of them.

(Welch, 1993: 1)

Four sets of general conclusions can be abstracted from this case study of GE's leadership system. These general conclusions group under three headings: critical success factors, the use of targets and implementing structures, and leadership skills and backbone communication processes.

(1) *Critical success factors for successful business leadership.* GE's three transformations reflect three different but interdependent goals which must be achieved to be a successful leader. *A*

leader must, first, position the firm in high-margin, high-growth product and service areas. If not, the firm will decline in value under his or her leadership. However, Welch's uniqueness is that he understood why and how that positioning had to be achieved. GE had to improve profits and improve stockholder value or market capitalization so as to become the most competitive and valued firm in the world. *A leader must, second, provide a firm with the leaders and management tools to become number one and fend off the challenge of other firms.* How was this to be achieved and why? Welch's answer was to create a boundaryless firm based on speed, simplicity, and candor. Only when leaders look outside themselves and move rapidly and decisively and with honesty can they adapt to the market changes caused by shifting consumer taste and competitor innovation and adaptation. Here, of course, leadership development programs, continuous-improvement programs, and rapid-response communication programs provide the necessary tools for meeting the threats caused by the need for rapid change. *A leader must third extend a firm's global reach.* How and why? By penetrating each of the world's major markets, employing the Internet to cut costs and increase speed, and linking all of a firm's stakeholders in the high-margin areas of service. Again it is Welch's uniqueness that he understood each of these three factors as necessary and collectively sufficient conditions for organizational success.

(2) **The use of targets and implementing structures.** Jack Welch and his leadership system is particularly skilled in providing appropriate targets and management tools for achieving these three organizational goals for success. Welch's uniqueness was that he provided clear multiple targets and that he indicated how to achieve them. Consider the targets which surrounded a business leader in the first transformation. The leader had to be number one or two in market shares in high-growth, high-margin areas; increase productivity, profits, and quality 15 percent per year; increase inventory turns to 6 per year; decentralize power downward; and carefully monitor the leaders under him or her and intervene to make them win-aholics. When these targets were achieved using GE's implementing structures, then the leader had succeeded in achieving the firm's goals.

(3) **The leadership skills and backbone communication processes necessary for success.** In all three transformation processes Jack Welch and all the leaders under him had to appropriately employ the six backbone communication processes or face failure in their attempts to achieve the critical success factors, meet

their targets, and effectively utilize their implementing structures and their management tools. In all three attempts at implementing change, Jack Welch and all the leaders under him manifested the six backbone skills of a transformational leader: (1) the anticipation of threat and thus a need to transform the firm in order to obtain a new environmental fit; (2) the creation and articulation of a clear and persuasive vision, targets, and implementing structures regarding how to reorient the firm's activities; (3) the creation of a tension in the firm's operating systems capable of halting its current operating activities; (4) the release of that tension by educating, providing management tools for, and empowering point people to lead change in a new adaptive direction; (5) the manifestation of productive results from the adaptation which can serve as a model or benchmark to others within the firm; and (6) the inculcation of a realization by a firm's members that this process must be repeated again and again. This backbone communication process is the engine driving the effective communication or organizational change.

In conclusion, perhaps the ABB benchmarking team which studied GE in 1994 put it best when they argued that Jack Welch and GE's success are accounted for by an effective communication system and a commitment to:

"• a vision that is credibly communicated and lived

• very tough performance targets set and communicated from the top

• rapid communication of information and decision making with limited analysis

• rapid implementation by empowered employees

• continuous push for improvement and change

• short feedback and learning cycles

• delegation and ownership to where it belongs"

(Harnischfeger, von der Weans, & Haven 1993).

In November 1999, Jack Welch, the CEO of General Electric for the past 19 years, announced that he would retire on April 1, 2000 (Deutsch 1999, C1). In December 2000, Welch announced he would remain CEO of GE until January 2001 in order to complete the Honeywell acquisition (Moore and Byrnes 2000, 95). A global search for Welch's replacement yielded three candidates from inside GE.

From 1999 to 2000, these leaders were rotated into problem areas to test their skills. In December 2001, Jeffrey Immelt, age 44, head of GE Medication Division, was named to replace Welch as CEO when he retired in 2002, once again testing the quality of GE's leadership training programs by locating a worthy replacement to the legendary Jack Welch.

References

Byrne, J. (1998). Jack: A close-up look at how America's #1 manager runs GE. *Business Week,* June 8, 92–104.

Carley, W. (1999). General Electric's first period net income rose 14 million dollars, *Wall Street Journal*, April 9, A4.

Case study: General Electric (1998). *Financial Times,* March 11, 20–21.

Colvin, G. (1999). The ultimate manager. *Fortune*, November 22, 185-187.

Corrigan, J. (1999). Reputations in business can be a fragile commodity. *Financial Times*, December 7, 1.

Deogun, N., and Scannell, E. (2000). Microsoft puts music into deals. *Wall Street Journal*, January 4, C1.

Deutsch, C. (1999). GE chief sets a date to step down. *New York Times*, November 3, C1.

Donion, J. (1993). Chief Executive of the Year: Alfred Sloan move over, *Chief Executive Magazine,* July/August, 1–8.

Flint, J. (1999). NBC is set to announce pact with broadband service firm Tolocity. *Wall Street Journal*, December 20, B9.

General Electric Company. (1992) Financial Affairs.www.GE.com

Grant, L. (1997). GE's Smart Bombing Strategy. *Fortune*, July 25, 190–110.

Hall, A., and Hargrave, D. (2001). Brussels Setback for GE-Honeywell Deal. *Financial Times*, February 28, 34.

Harnischfeger, F., von der Weans, G., and Haven, T. (1993). General Electric—A company for ABB to learn from? *ABB Benchmarking Study,* November.

Henry, D. (1997). GE chief takes well-read look into future. *USA Today*, February 21, 7B.

———. (1998). GE's Welch sees opportunities in Asia Crises. *USA Today*, February 27, 8B.

Hill, A. (1999). Welch bullish on outlook for GE. *Financial Times,* December 13, 23.

Hyatt, J. and Naj, J. (1992). GE is no place for autocrats, Welch decrees. *Wall Street Journal,* March 3, B1.

Immelt, J. (2001). *GE's 2001 Annual Report to Our Share Owners, Customers, and Employers.*

————. *GE Annual Report 2001.* www.ge.annual 2001.

Kahn, J. (1998). The Fortune Global 500. *Fortune,* August 3, 130–F29.

Kerr, S. (1988). Risky business: The new pay game. *Fortune,* July 22, 93–96.

King S. and Cushman, D. (eds.) (1994). *High-Speed Management and Organizational Communication in the 1990s: A Reader.* Albany: State University of New York Press.

————. (1995). Leading organizational change: A high-speed management perspective. In *Communicating Change: A Management Perspective,* ed. D. Cushman and S.S. King. Albany: State University of New York Press.

Koenig, P. (1996). If Europe's dead, why is GE investing billions there? *Fortune,* September 9, 114-118.

Microsoft drops to No. 3 in value behind GE (1999). *Palm Beach Post,* November 17, 7B.

Moore, P. and Brady, D. (2000). Running the house that Jack built. *Business Week,* October 2, 130.

Moore, P., and Byrnes, N. (2000). The man who would be Welch. *Business Week.* December 11, 94–96.

Murray, M (1998). GE Capital goes bargain hunting in troubled Asia. *Wall Street Journal,* March 12, B4.

————. (1999a). Late to the Web, GE now views Internet as key to growth. *Wall Street Journal,* June 22, B1.

————. (1999b). GE's next generation prepares for life without Jack. *Wall Street Journal,* August 3, B1.

————. (2001). GE profits rise 16% but Welch warns of layoffs. *Wall Street Journal,* January 18, A3.

Pope, K. (1999). NBC plans to buy stake in Value Vision to expand Internet retailing presence. *New York Times,* March 10, B6.

Rao, S. (2000). General Electric software vendor. *Forbes,* January 24, 144–146.

Sapsford, J. (1999a). GE Capital buys $7 billion in Japanese firms. *Wall Street Journal,* January 25, A13.

————. (1999b). GE moves to let consumers receive, pay bills from credit card issuer online. *Wall Street Journal,* December 14, A4.

Siklos, R., and Brady, D. (1999). NBC dealing itself into E-commerce. *Business Week*, October 4, 42.

Smart, T. (1993). Jack Welch on the art of thinking small. *Business Week Enterprise,* 212–216.

———. (1996). Jack Welch's encore. *Business Week*, October 28, 155–160.

Smart, T., Engardio, P., and Smith, G.A. (1993). GE's brave new world. *Business Week*, November 8, 64–70.

Smart, T., Templeton, J., and Dwyer P. (1995). GE Capital's grand tour of Europe. *Business Week*, October 16, 62.

Stark, G. (1988). Time: The next source of competitive advantage. *Harvard Business Review*, July/August 41–51.

Stewart, T. (1991). GE keeps those ideas coming. *Fortune*, August 12, 118–122.

———. (1992). The firm of tomorrow. *Fortune*, May 18, 93–98.

———. (1993). Reengineering: The hot new managing tool. *Fortune*, August 23, 41–48.

———. (1999). See Jack, See Jack run Europe. *Fortune*, September 27, 124–136.

Tichy, N. M. and Charon, P. (1989). Speed, simplicity, and self-confidence: An interview with Jack Welch. *Harvard Business Review*, September/October 112–120.

Welch, J. (1988). Managing for the nineties. *GE Speech Reprint.*

———. (1991). In pursuit of speed. *GE Speech Reprints,* April 24.

———. (1993a). Jack Welch's lessons for success. *Fortune*, January 25, 96–94.

———. (1993b). The speed and spirit of a boundaryless company, *GE Speech Reprints*, April 28, 1–4.

———. (1997). *Letter to Shareholders.* February 21.

Womack, J., Jones, D., and Roos, M. (1990). How lean production can change the world. *The New York Times Magazine*, September 23, 22–37.

Workout, GE Publication, 1–10, September 1991.

Wu Dunn, S. (1999). Capitalizing on Asian doldrums. *New York Times*, September 14, C1.

4

Best Practices at the Microsoft Corporation: Benchmarking a World-Class Marketing Communication System

I personally believe that Microsoft is the most powerful eco-nomic force in the United States in the second half of the 20th century. Some of Microsoft's control over competing, at all lev-els, is obvious. Much, however, is invisible. Even longtime in-siders are just beginning to understand the nature of that power, how Microsoft acquired it, preserves it, and exercises it.

(Schmidt, 1996:B1)

The Microsoft Corporation is considered by most observers to be one of the most competitive firms in the world. In 2000, Microsoft became the most valued firm in America with $525 billion in stock-holder investments. In 1999, Microsoft was selected in polls con-ducted by the European *Financial Times* as the most innovative firm in the world and in 1998 by the U.S. *Fortune Magazine* as second to the General Electric Company as the most admired firm in America (Stewart 1998, 71). Between 1975 and 2001 Microsoft went from a two-person firm with $16,000 in sales to one of the world's most powerful corporations with 30,000 employees, $25.296 billion in sales, and over $7.346 billion in profits (*Fortune 500* 2001, F49). In that same time frame, Bill Gates, the CEO of Microsoft, went from being a Harvard dropout to amassing a $87 billion fortune from his 20 percent shares of Microsoft stock. In addition, six Microsoft employ-ees had become billionaires and 2,800 had become millionaires based on their holdings of Microsoft (Hamm, Cortese, and Burrows 1998, G2). Microsoft, it would appear, is a remarkable example of an American success story.

In spite of this success, Microsoft's competitors within the software market see a different Microsoft. They speak of Microsoft's

Table 4.1
Microsoft's Seven-Year Performance Record: 1995–2001
(in millions of dollars)

Microsoft	2001	2000	1999	1998	1997	1996	1995
Sales	25,296	22,956	21,855	14,484	11,360	8,670	5,940
Profits	7,346	9,421	8,746	4,490	3,450	2,200	1,450

Source: Microsoft Corporation, "Financial Facts" (www.Microsoft.com, 2002)

"will to dominate" with concern and fear and as a threat to those firms' very survival. Michael Kapar, CEO of Lotus Development Corporation, argues, "The question of what to do about Microsoft is going to be a central public policy issue for the next 20 years. Policymakers don't understand the real character of Microsoft yet—the sheer will-to-power that Microsoft has" (Gleick 1995, 39). Lawrence Ellison, CEO of Oracle, another Microsoft competitor asserts that "Bill Gates and Microsoft do not just want to compete in the computer industry. Rather, they seek to dominate every aspect of the market, to eliminate their competition" (Cortese et. al. 1995, 86). Several of Microsoft's competitors, including IBM, Sun Micro Systems, and Netscape, have banded together and asked the U.S., European Union, and Japanese governments to investigate Microsoft's marketing practices for using their monopolistic position in PC operating systems to illegally restrain trade in the software industry. By April 2000, the U.S. inquiry into Microsoft's marketing practices had determined that Microsoft did violate U.S. antitrust laws and began reviewing the most appropriate actions for dealing with these violations (Wilke 2000, Al). By April 2001, the inquiry was under review by a three-man board which was considering setting aside the 2000 ruling as inappropriate given the evidence presented.

It will be the purpose of this chapter to benchmark Microsoft's best practices in marketing in order to understand both the legal and illegal aspects of the company's strategies and practices. In so doing, we will explore Microsoft's marketing position and the critical success factors and backbone communication processes of its marketing strategies. We will benchmark the company's 1998–1999 competition with the Oracle Corporation for control of the database software market, and finally draw some conclusions regarding our inquiry. Let us explore each of these in turn.

Microsoft's Market Position

If the wolf comes, what happens to the sheep?

(Chang, 1999:B1)

Each day one billion people throughout the world use personal computers, 880 million of them begin by entering the Microsoft Windows operating system, and 900 million of them select one of Microsoft's applications to begin their work. Microsoft holds a dominant position in each of these software markets. Microsoft's operating profit margin in 1999 was a remarkable 52 percent, one of the highest in any industry (Nee 1999, 12).

By June 2001, Microsoft had six major software products and held varying market shares for each. Microsoft's first product is *office applications*. Here Microsoft's Office Suite had 92 percent of global market shares. Microsoft's second product is a *PC operating system*. Here Microsoft's Windows held 91 percent of the world's market share. Microsoft's third product is *Internet browsers*. Here Microsoft held 75 percent of global market shares. Microsoft's fourth product is *Internet servers*. Here Microsoft's NT servers held 41 percent of the world's market shares. Microsoft's fifth product is *handheld computer operating systems*. Here Microsoft's CE held 34 percent of the global market. Microsoft's sixth product is a *database operating system*. Here Microsoft's SQL-7 held 14.9 percent of global market shares (Harmon 2001, C1; Buckman and Gomes 2001, 135). Notice that Microsoft's latter three products were in markets they did not dominate, but were employing their famed marketing practices to increase market shares in the hope of gaining a dominant position (Harmon 2001, 61).

In 1997, the Netscape Corporation held 62 percent of the browser market and Microsoft had a 36 percent market share. Jim Clark, CEO of Netscape, asked the U.S. government to investigate Microsoft's marketing practices for employing its monopolistic position in PC operating systems to leverage its increasing market share in Internet browsers and servers. Legally a 70 percent market share is defined by law as a monopolistic position. However, having a monopolistic position is not illegal. What is illegal is using that position to restrain free trade in another market. Three years later, in 2000, the courts ruled in favor of Netscape's claims. However, Jim Clark said, "It's done, over. Microsoft had achieved what it set out to do" (Bank 2000:B1). Netscape sold its firm to American On-Line in the hopes of halting its market share decline.

Attention is now directed to understanding Microsoft's marketing strategy, critical success factors, and backbone communication processes.

Marketing Strategy, Critical Success Factors, and Backbone Communication Processes

In Corporate America, does it get much better than this? Imagine a 24-year old company still hotfooting along like some young whippersnapper. Revenues and profits rising at a 30% clip. Income per employee is an enviable $257,000, vs. an average of $17,000 for the Standard and Poor's 500-stock index. And the company has gone on a spending spree, investing in or gobbling up 92 companies in the past five years. Still, it has $92 billion in cash—more than any other corporation in the U.S. Oh yeah—it also boasts the highest market cap of the lot, $414 billion.

(Moeller, Hamm, Mullaney, May 17, 1999:106)

Microsoft's products and services are aimed at empowering people and organizations by providing them with an easy way of finding and using information. In order to compete successfully in the software industry, Bill Gates believes that Microsoft's organizational goal must be to "pioneer and orchestrate evolving mass markets" (Cusumano and Selby 1995, 127). In so doing Gates hopes to bring Microsoft closer to his grand vision in which Microsoft's software will run on any device, easily connecting people to the Internet wherever they happen to be (Greene 2001, 75). Microsoft employs five critical success factors and four backbone communication processes in attempting to meet this goal.

Microsoft's Critical Success Factors

1. Enter evolving mass markets early or stimulate new markets with good products which can become the industry standard.

2. Continuously improve products incrementally and periodically make old products obsolete.

3. Push volume sales to ensure that products become and remain the industry standard.

4. Leverage the industrial standard to develop new products and market linkages.

5. Integrate, extend, and simplify products and services to reach new mass markets. (Cusumano and Selby, 1995, 127)

Two of these five critical success factors require an extended analysis in order to understand Microsoft's operations: the benefits of its continuous-improvement program and its focus on the setting of industrial standards.

The Benefits of Continuous Improvement
Developing a "good" product in the software industry is a complex activity. It involves working within several rather fixed and important parameters. *First*, there are technological parameters to the hardware, that is, what the basic architecture of the hardware can do. *Second*, there are historical parameters involving past applications, operating systems, and marketing segments which must be preserved in a new program to maintain or expand a mass market. *Third*, there are emerging areas for new operating systems, applications, and market segments needed to create or maintain a mass market. *Fourth*, there are the strengths and weaknesses of various interface capabilities between these parameters and their users. *Finally*, computer software is a rapidly evolving business where in three years all the products, services, and knowledge we have today may be outdated; thus timing in getting to market a product which fits all these stakeholder needs is a challenge.

In order to successfully navigate all these important parameters plus the normal volatility in the global economy of unexpected competition, quick market saturation, and technological breakthroughs, it is necessary to get products out in the market and then use one's resources as a large, financially sound, and rapidly responding firm to develop or acquire existing or new technologies in order to meet your stakeholder needs more effectively than your competitors. That is why most initial software offerings are not industry leaders. Rather, through continuous improvement, on the fifth or eighth try they achieve the status of industrial standards. That happened with Q-DOS, MS-DOS, Windows, Office Suite, and so forth.

A Focus on Setting Industry Standards
The age of mass production for mass markets could not begin until the world agreed on standards for nuts, bolts, and parts, and their

interface. Establishing standards acts as a catalyst for developing mass markets. In the past, many of these standards were set by governments, international organizations, or industry consortia, but seldom by a single firm. The more complex the products, the more precise the standards must be, and computer software is a very complex product. In understanding the two-decade history of Microsoft's increasing control over the computer industry, nothing matters more than its strategic management of the creation and manipulation of standards.

It works like this. In order to successfully work within all the parameters for creating software listed above, all the key players in an area of the industry must meet and negotiate a common standard which includes the integration of their past, current, and future products and technologies. Let us say you are an expert in a small firm in voice recognition and involved in turning that recognition into a printed text. One day you get an invitation from Microsoft to come to meetings on standards. You cannot not go or your products and interests could be excluded. Then, under Microsoft's guidance, you and several other firms negotiate the rules governing the API, or applications program interface. Not many large software firms have the power to call such a set of meetings, but Microsoft does. The result of these meetings is that Microsoft, in cooperation with virtually the entire speech software industry, released the Microsoft Speech Software Development Kit containing all the necessary tools to develop applications which meet the standards set. The problem of setting new standards which will create a mass market is solved. However, in these standards meetings, Microsoft receives and files away an enormous body of intelligence on the speech software industry. It discovers where the competitors have been, where they are going, and how they will get there. It then has the competitive intelligence necessary to develop a balanced software program for meeting the complexities of the parameters in a given area. Microsoft has held such conferences on standards in the area of e-mail, network integration, multimedia applications, and so forth. Microsoft is not the only firm attempting to set standards, but it is one of the largest and most effective at doing so.

Cusumano and Selby (1995, 163) in their seminal study of Microsoft's competitive effectiveness summarizes our analysis when they argue,

> Microsoft's goal was emphatically not the maximization of revenue or even market share; it was creating relationships with customers, software developers and microprocessor firms like

Intel to give as many reasons as possible to support—strategically, financially, and technically—Microsoft's operating systems. These networks of relationships are what makes a standard something more than a product. The standard is not the product of a company, it's the byproduct of these networks. Managing standards means managing networks.

What happens if you support Microsoft in setting these standards? Many firms prosper. Intel, Compaq, and others have profited immensely. And what happens if you oppose Microsoft's standards and support a competing standard? Again, some firms prosper, as Sun and Oracle have by setting their own Internet operating systems and database standards. However, other firms have dramatically lost market shares as in the case of Lotus 1-2-3 Spreadsheet, Borland International's Paradox, Netscape's Explorer, and IBM's OS/2 operating system. Standards confer near monopoly power in most areas of computer software. In 1995, several banking and networking firms asked the U.S. government to examine Microsoft's competitive strategies in setting standards as a possible violation of the antitrust laws. However, evidence was hard to come by since almost all competing firms in the industry had some type of alliance, joint venture, or licensing agreement with Microsoft and realized that Microsoft is a good friend and a bad enemy. This led some observers of the software industry, like Jerry Kaplan, a former Lotus executive, to argue, "What we need in the software business is a witness protection program" (Schlender and Kirkpatrick 1995, 90).

Backbone Communication Processes

Microsoft employs four backbone communication processes in support of its five critical success factors.

(1) *The product development and continuous improvement linkage to Microsoft's unique brand of teamwork.* To manage creative people and technical skills in an efficient manner, and to produce new and continuously improved products in a manner that sets the industry standard, Microsoft employs a unique form of teamwork. This form of teamwork established functional specialties within small modular teams with overlapping responsibilities. Product managers, software developers, and testers are the main functional specialists within a product unit:

> Within the product unit, program managers, developers and testers work side by side in small "feature teams" These typically consist of one program manager, three to eight developers,

and a parallel features testing band whose members are paired with developers (Cusumano and Selby 1995, 74).

In addition each product team also includes product managers who are marketing specialists, customer support engineers who provide technical assistance to users and analyze customer feedback, a user education staff which prepares manuals and helps with documentation, and actual customers who will use the software.

Program managers can lead several features teams, and product managers can lead several program teams. Group and division managers supervise and review all program and product teams' progress. Bill Gates supervises and reviews all group and division leader efforts. Such parallel and synchronous teams with overlapping functional responsibilities and multiple layers of review have several unique competitive advantages. First, they are self-correcting based on overlapping functions, parallel synchronization, customer and stakeholder feedback, and multiple levels of review. Second, they can be expanded, contracted, eliminated, and redirected quickly due to their modular structure. Third, representation on such teams is uniquely weighted in favor of the marketplace demands of customers. When parallel programming and testing functions are guided by the competitive intelligence gained from the API standards meetings, then Microsoft can take an initial product offering and transform it through upgrades to a market standard which better meets customer and stakeholder parameters than its competitors. When the largest reported item on such a team is from marketing sales and customers, then voting is weighted in favor of the customer.

(2) The setting of industrial standards linkage to Microsoft's unique acquisitions, product development, and alliances policies. Central to setting industrial interface and product standards is state-of-the-art technology and strong partners who will support the standards which Microsoft puts forward. Microsoft's alliances with Intel, the leading PC chip manufacturer in the world, and Compaq, the leading PC manufacturer in the United States, provides a strong foundation for setting or opposing other firms' attempts to set standards in the PC market. It would be hard to conceive of a stronger, more influential set of partners for establishing PC standards, and similar strong alliances exist in other areas.

(3) The volume marketing and distribution linkage to competitive pricing, exclusive contracting, and software bundling. Volume sales are critically important to the competitiveness of a software firm. Bill Gates tells why: "It's all about scale economies and market share. When you're shipping a million units of Windows software a month,

you can afford to spend $300 million a year improving it and still sell it at a low price" (Cusumano and Selby 1995, 158). Executive vice president of Microsoft Steve Ballmer elaborates: "Software businesses are all fixed cost businesses. And so volume is absolutely everything . . . because you have to amortize that fixed cost very broadly" (Cusumano and Selby 1995, 158). The result is that no PC software firm can match Microsoft's financial resources. The company spent over $1 billion plus on R & D in 1999 and has salted away $19 billion for acquisitions and joint ventures.

Windows 95 and Windows 98 used aggressive pricing, licensing, and contract tactics to obtain volume sales. Windows 95 sold at retail outlets for about $95.00. For high volume wholesalers, it sold at about $35. For hardware makers the price could be reduced to about $30, if they agreed to preinstall Windows 95 on 50 percent or more of their PC shipments and adopt the Windows 95 logo (Cusumano and Selby 1995, 161). Thanks to such preinstallation contracts, Windows 95 was preloaded on 70 percent of all PCs sold in 1995 and Windows XP 2000 was preloaded on 97 percent of all PCs sold in 2001.

In addition to volume-purchase price reductions and preshipment installation contracts, Microsoft developed a competitive strategy called "applications bundling." Microsoft Office Suite features an integration of the most commonly used desktop applications word processing (Microsoft Word), business spreadsheets (Microsoft Excel), computer graphics (Microsoft PowerPoint), database management (Microsoft ACCESS), and e-mail (Microsoft Hot Mail) into a single package selling for about $250. Retail price for each of the products in Office Suite sold independent was about $300 each. Once again further price reductions were possible with preshipment installation contracts. Many hardware providers signed such contracts, The net effect of such bundling and reshipment contracts is that each of these independent products leads its software category in sales.

The effect on competitors was devastating. Word Perfect, Lotus 1,2,3, and others had led the word processing and spreadsheet market, but Microsoft's Office Suite reduced their market shares to close to nothing, placing the firms in financial jeopardy. Microsoft has employed pricing, preshipment contracts, and bundling in the desktop publishing, multimedia, shop floor automation, and home, banking, and computer games applications markets. The company's use of these tactics has served to create mass markets for Microsoft in a manner that limits its competitors' capacity to compete, helping to create a sustainable competitive advantage for Microsoft products.

(4) Leveraging standards to limit competitors' sales and link Microsoft products to new mass markets. Three examples will serve to

illustrate Microsoft's use of this strategy. Cusumano and Selby (1995, 160) wrote,

> Digital Research, CPI M-86 (developed in the early 1980s) might have become the dominant PC operating system; reportedly, it had better memory management features and other advantages over MS-DOS. Microsoft, however, was the leading language producer, and it did not rush to deliver versions of its languages compatible with CP/M86. When it did ship compatible languages, Microsoft priced them 50 percent over DOS-compatible versions, and they sold in low volumes. Microsoft also sold an inferior version of Basic, stripped of graphics. As a result, applications developers found it difficult to write anything but MS-DOS, and CP/M-86 failed as a competing product.

Windows 95 contains an icon and input capability for accessing Microsoft online, a network feature of the program. When a Windows user employed the icon, access was obtained to both Microsoft online and the World Wide Web. When a user employs another online service for the linkage to Windows 95, the program disconnects the input system and makes it inoperable. Microsoft's competitors who are network providers filed a restraint of trade claim against Microsoft for the Windows 95 disconnect function (Cusumano and Selby 1995, 181).

Finally, when one PC operating system controls 91 percent of the PC market, most independent firms writing PC applications programs will find it most lucrative to develop their products first for compatibility with that system. Then if time and resources permit, the firms will be developing applications for competing systems. Windows 95, 98, and XP 2000 are so dominant in the PC market that most software development firms do not write Mac OS and OS/2 applications for their products because the market shares are too small to warrant the effort. Both Apple and IBM have had and continue to have trouble getting independent software firms to write applications for their operating systems. Firms that provide operating systems with a limited number of applications have trouble selling those systems. The result is that Windows 95 comes preinstalled on all Apple and IBM computers along with each firm's own operating system. This prevents Apple and IBM from making a serious attempt to increase its market shares and limits the sale of their own hardware systems. In addition, Microsoft was having trouble getting independent software firms to write application programs for its Windows NT workstations operating systems. It solved the problem by requiring every firm which developed a program for Windows 95, 98, or XP 2000 by contract to deliver the same program adapted to the Windows NT architecture. As a result, Windows NT has the most extensive applications library of any operating system.

We have reviewed four of Microsoft's backbone communication linkages between its critical success factors and their tactical operationalization at the worker/market interface: (1) the product development and continuous-improvement linkages to teamwork; (2) the setting of industrial standards linkage to acquisitions and alliances; (3) the volume marketing and distribution linkages to pricing, contracting, and software bundling; and (4) leveraging standards to limit competitor sales and link Microsoft products to mass markets. In each area, these backbone communication processes are employed to provide Microsoft with a sustainable competitive advantage over other firms. Attention is now directed to Microsoft's position with the Oracle software firm for control of the database market.

Benchmarking Microsoft's Competition with the Oracle Corporation in the Database Software Market

The $9.5 billion a year data base market grew 10% last year, a respectable rise for a product that has been around 20 years. So how is it that once promising players, Sybase and Informix, have been struggling and Oracle, the market leader, warns of tough times a head? The answer in a word: Microsoft. Microsoft is roiling the data-base business with cutthroat pricing, product bundling and sweet deals for customers and software developers—the same tactics by which it dominated PC software, earned the enmity of competitors and provoked a bitter U.S. antitrust lawsuit that charges Microsoft in effect with the crime of giving consumers too good a deal.

(Pitta, 1999:21-22)

Table 4.2 lists the major participants as of December 1998 in the database software market, their relative market shares, and the growth in those market shares for that year.

Table 4.2
1998 Database

%	Oracle	IBM	Microsoft	Informix	Sybase	Others
Market share	43	15	6	6	4	26
Growth Over 1997	21	24	35	9	−13	—

Source: *International Data,* 1998.

The database market consists of three computer segments: mainframes, midrange, and servers. Oracle and IBM have software programs in all three segments. Informix and Sybase have software in the midrange segments. Microsoft SQL-7 software operates in the server market only on Microsoft NT servers. Oracle's database software programs operate on both Unix servers and on Microsoft's NT servers. Table 4.3 shows the 1997 database market shares for the two major segments of the server market.

Table 4.3
1997 Market Shares in the Two Major Segments
of the Server Market

	Oracle	IBM	Microsoft	Others
Unix Systems	61%	7%	0%	32%
Windows NT	47%	10%	3%	13%

Source: *International Data,* 1997.

In 1998 and 1999, the competition between Oracle and Microsoft was for control of the database market in servers. Oracle 8 was a software program for all segments of the server market and sold for $300 to $500 depending on add-ons. Microsoft's SQL-7 program for NT servers sold for between $50 and $100 and also came as part of Microsoft's back office suite at even less cost. Oracle 8 was a faster, leaner, larger, more flexible, and more stable program. In addition, Oracle 8 ran on all the major software operating systems including Microsoft, Unix and Linus, and Java and KML, the three major Internet systems. Microsoft, which had a price advantage, ran only on its NT servers and not on Unix and Linus servers. Oracle, with 47 percent of the NT market share, compared to Microsoft's 41 percent market share, and 61 percent of the Unix market, along with its speed, scale, flexibility, and stability, would seem to hold a significant and dominant position in the database software market for servers.

Benchmarking Microsoft's 1998–1999 Competition with Oracle for Control of the Server Database Market

Microsoft rules the desktop in PC software, while its share of data base programs on servers seems small for now. But its blistering sales growth there has sent lesser entrants seeking protective niches and put it in position to challenge IBM. Next up Oracle.

(Pitta, 1999:22)

We will benchmark Microsoft's and Oracle's 1998–1999 performance in the database software market by exploring Microsoft's four backbone communication linkages to its five critical success factors in marketing. We will then explore Oracle's strategies in responding to Microsoft's efforts.

1. The product development, continuous-improvement linkage to Microsoft's unique brand of teamwork

Aware of the serious technical shortcomings of its SQL-7 data base software, in 1995 Microsoft began a bold development program called Windows XP 2000 aimed at correcting these shortcomings. This new operating system was in fact four different operating systems under one name. *The first operating system* was Windows XP 2000 for NT servers. This program had many unique features, the most significant of which was to allow the parallel linking and processing of NT servers to create databases of any size, from mainframe capabilities to simple server size. *The second operating system,* for professionals, included business desktops and notebooks. Its most important features included its flexibility and stability. It can multitask and is designed not to crash. *The third operating system* is for advanced servers or e-commerce. Its most important features include the storage and use of software applications on the server and its ability to use Internet operating systems languages. Each of these three Windows XP 2000 operating systems was released in February of 2000. *The fourth operating system* for Windows XP 2000 is for database servers. This systems was released in November of 2000. Its most important features are its flexibility, stability, scaling, and openness to other operating systems. It was designed to run 7000 user applications increasing its flexibility, to limit significantly its likelihood of crashing, to work on all Internet operating systems and workstations and servers at speeds that exceed Oracle 8. Microsoft committed 4000 programmers to developing Windows XP 2000 and employed the company's unique brand of teamwork in developing and testing the operating system (Price 2000, 33).

New product developments like Windows XP 2000 create good and bad news. The good news is that in February and March of the year 2000 these new products made Microsoft more competitive in these four areas of operating systems. The bad news is that throughout 1998 and 1999 sales slowed in anticipation of Windows XP 2000 for upgrading computers. Table 4.4 reflects that sales reality.

Table 4.4
Market Shares for Servers Operating Systems, 1998–1999

New Units	Windows NT	Linux	Unix
1998: 4.4 million	38%	16%	19%
1999: 5.4 million	38%	25%	15%
Growth: Total Sold	+23%	+73%	+1.4%

Source: J. Markoff, "Windows 2000 facing a skeptical market," *New York Times,* February 14, 2000.

Between 2000 and 2002, Microsoft's XP 2000 is expected to extend its market shares in all four markets for which Windows 2000 is designed (Bank 2000, B8; Wildstrom 2000, 20).

Oracle does not employ development teams strongly weighted in favor of the customer. The company views such a marketing strategy as reactive. It employs a proactive strategy. Oracle believes that its development staff knows the directions in which the database market is heading, understands the available technology, and develops its operating systems so as to be on the cutting edge, and then must educate customers to the systems' advantages and appropriate use. Oracle 8 ran on all major operating systems and was technically superior in flexibility, scalability, and stability to Microsoft's SQL-7. Oracle's major continuous-improvement programs in 1998 and 1999 focused on cutting $4 billion from its operating budget by 2001 by shifting all operations to the Internet. This involves consolidating its 70 databases in 70 locations to one online database—the putting in place of an Internet store for marketing all its products and services. Two highly anticipated products from Oracle were the suite of software that will help build Web-based operations and the creation of a free software and service technology Netwide. The technology portal already has signed up 500,000 developers as members since January 1999 (Iwata 1999, 4B). Oracle has also assigned 2,000 additional sales staff to push the development sales of applications. Oracle supported this effort with an increase to $500 million of its investment in conferences and seminars for applications development (Iwata 1999, 4B). Finally, Oracle committed a large portion of its sales staff to focus on two needed development projects. The fist was aimed at selling Internet sites to all the Fortune 100 firms. The second was to approach the three largest firms in each global business market and asked them to link together in establishing a business-to-business bazaar Internet site for parts and services. These two initiatives would force all smaller firms who supply these Fortune 100 firms and who participate in these industry bazaars to employ similar database software and lead to a geometric increase in Oracle's sales. All of this was predicated on a rapid rise in Internet sites by large firms (Greene 2000, 34).

By January of 2000, Oracle could boast that its database software was utilized by 9 of the 10 largest Internet sites based on sales, and 65 of the Fortune 100 firms, and that they were near completion of six agreements to set up industry bazaar sites in the auto, department store, chemical, health care, aerospace, and financial services markets (Greene 2000, 34).

2. The Setting of Industrial Standards Linkages to Microsoft's Unique Acquisitions, Product Development, and Alliance Policies

Prior to the appearance of Windows XP 2000, Microsoft's SQL-7 database software was limited in its applications to NT servers. In January of 1998, Microsoft held 30 percent of that market while Oracle held 47 percent. Microsoft's direct object then was to upgrade its SQL-7 across its NT servers in the hope of gaining software market shares to set the standard. To encourage this process, Microsoft was moving rapidly to e-commerce independent programs and consulting firms to develop applications for and encourage the use of SQL-7. Microsoft allocated $600 million in 1998 and even more in 1999 to sponsor conferences and workshops, and to provide consultants to support such firms' activities. In 1998, over 2,000 firms were brought on board the SQL-7 software train through this process (Pitta 1999, 22; Bank 1998, A6). Microsoft also has $19 billion in cash for investment in firms which support these SQL-7 efforts (Pitta 1999, 22).

This effort did achieve some notable success. Microsoft convinced firms like Burger King; HBO & Co., the largest seller of health care management software; and Harper Collins Publishing to shift from Oracle to SQL-7. All four firms cited price and Microsoft's support system as their primary motivation. In each case Microsoft provided 3 to 4 months of free technical support worth $30,000 to $50,000 in order to adapt the program to the firm's specific investment needs (Banks 2000: A6). Microsoft spent $20 million in 1998 to train over 50,000 database administrators for corporate clients. Similarly, Microsoft went out of its way to wine, dine, and train independent programming, consulting, and Information technology officers.

Oracle was very active in attempting to set the standard in database software and link that to their acquisition, product development and alliance policies. Oracle conducted major advertising campaigns through 1998 and 1999, announcing that their software was used by 9 of the 10 largest Internet sites and 65 of the Fortune 100 Internet sites, and describing its attempt to form B2B Internet bazaars. In addition, Oracle set aside $100 million to invest in firms which aimed to advance their effort. In 1998, it invested $28 million in such firms and obtained a 500 percent return on their investments. In 1999, Oracle invested in 70 firms to encourage Linux and Unix servers (Gomes 2000, B4). Oracle was also able to pick up several former SQL-7 users whose databases outgrew SQL-7 size or suffered from stability problems (Bank 1998, B4).

3. The Volume Marketing and Distribution Link to Competitive Pricing, Exclusive Contracts, and Software Bundling

Microsoft has long practiced low pricing, exclusive contracting, and software bundling, and the database market is no exception. SQL-7 has been sold for as little as $50 and one half of that for customers who discontinue the use of Oracle 8. SQL-7 is also bundled with Microsoft's back office suite which further lowers its price. To compete with this low pricing strategy Oracle has ordered its sales staff to match Microsoft's price on low-end services but hold its price on high-end services. This allows Microsoft to put pressure on Oracle in the server market. Between 1998 and 2001, Microsoft's market shares in the NT server market climbed from 30 percent to 42 percent while Oracle's market shares went from 42 percent to 40 percent, with IBM losing ground also to Microsoft (Data Quest 2001).

In early 1998 Microsoft persuaded SAP-AG, the leading vendor of software that runs entire businesses, to bundle SQL-7 and later Windows XP 2000 for business centers with all its own software. Oracle 8 was also involved in this bundling process. This does, however, indicate a growing demand among SAP-AG customers for SQL-7 (Bank 1998).

4. The Leveraging of Industrial Standards to Limit Competition, Linking Microsoft's Products to New Mass Markets

While Microsoft's SQL-7 is limited in use to NT servers, the firm is trying to migrate its software across NT servers with some success—an 8 percent gain in market shares over two years. However, the advance advertising on Windows XP 2000 for data centers has led many customers to wait the arrival of this new product.

Meanwhile, Oracle has been very successful in leveraging its program's use to sell its products to firms who interact with these sites. Equally important is Oracle's move into B2B Bazaar sales, which has a similar high payoff once large industries establish such bazaars (Coleman and Woodruff 2000, A4).

By June of 2000, Oracle's worldwide database market share stood at 33.8 percent while Microsoft's overall share was 14.9 percent (Buckman and Gomes 2001, B5).

Conclusions

Oracle Chairman Lawrence J. Ellison likes to boast that his company figured out the Internet revolution long before competitors knew what a browser was. He crows that nine of the top ten corporate Web sites use Oracle data base software as a foundation. And now Ellison has something else to brag about.

With two deals, Oracle put itself at the nexus of what could become one of the biggest and potentially most lucrative bets on the Net yet, B2B bazaars. . . . Oracle announced a new auto parts exchange by the big three—Ford, GM, Mercedes Chrysler—and a retail business bazaar in Sears and Carrefour of Paris.

(Greene, 2000:34)

The most dramatic difference between Microsoft's and Oracle's backbone communication processes in marketing strategy appears in the development of new products:

(1) ***The product development, continuous-improvement linkage to Microsoft's unique brand of teamwork.*** Here Microsoft employs a *reactive strategy* rooted in Microsoft's unique form of teamwork which is designed to respond to customer needs. Oracle on the other hand employs a *proactive strategy* of designing open systems software that anticipates the customer's needs and then educates the customer to the advantages of Oracle's products. This allows Oracle to lead while Microsoft must wait and react to the market.

In regard to the other three strategies employed by Microsoft, Oracle uses all of them, and perhaps more effectively at this point in time, than Microsoft.

(2) The setting of industrial standards linkage to Microsoft's unique acquisition, product development, and alliance policies.

(3) The volume marketing and distribution link to computer pricing, exclusive contracting, and software bundling.

(4) The leveraging of industrial standards to limit competition, linking Microsoft products to new mass markets.

Between 1998 and 2000, Oracle was clearly the superior performer. However, with the appearance of Windows XP 2000 for data centers in November of 2000, the competition moved to a new level. Microsoft could then compete with Oracle in all its database markets as a technological equal. This will put continued pressure on their differences in marketing strategy. Microsoft will once again be late to market with an equal product, but will, as it has in the past, attempt to dominate. In long and extended competitions, Microsoft's size, 40,000 programs, and superior resources, $19 billion for acquisitions, R & D and so forth, have served it well. Several firms have held 60 to 70 percent market shares at one point in time and then had to withdraw from the market at another. IBM with OS/2, Cornell with Word Perfect, Lotus with 1,2,3, and Netscape with its browser and servers at one point in time had a technical and market share lead on Microsoft, only to lose their technical and market shares to a dominant and monopolistic Microsoft product. Time will tell if this occurs again. Oracle's strategy of focusing on large systems which are expensive and difficult to change and putting pressure on all firms who interact with these large systems to develop similar and compatible software has geometric implications for Oracle's sales to small and medium-size firms on the Internet and may in the long run be the superior force.

Finally, technological change is so rapid, there is considerable doubt if government regulations and court cases can respond in time to matter. While the U.S. government has decided that Microsoft violated antitrust laws, the government is completely at a loss as to what to do about it. Both the government and the firms that launched the suit feel that it may be too late, short of a fine, to matter. In addition, it may take several more years of appeal before a viable solution will emerge without Microsoft agreeing to a settlement (France et al. 1999, 4). In the meantime, Microsoft's world-class marketing system carries on, advancing market shares in each of its product categories until Microsoft is dominant.

References

Bank, D. (1998). Why Oracle is having fits with an upstart known as Microsoft. *Wall Street Journal*, July 24, A1, A6.

———. (2000). Microsoft and market expects slower start for Windows 2000 sales. *Wall Street Journal*, February 14, B8.

Binkley, J. (1999). Finding fault with Microsoft. *New York Times*, November 6, B1.

Buckman, R. (2002). Microsoft posts hefty 18% revenue rise. *Wall Street Journal*, January 18, A4.

Buckman, R., and Gomes L. (2001). Oracle unveils database, Kills pricing plan. *Wall Street Journal*, June 15, B5.

Coleman, C., and Woodruff, D. (2000). Sears, Carrefour plan to create Web exchange. *Wall Street Journal*, February 29, A4.

Corporate Scoreboard (2000). *Business Week,* February 28, 117.

Cortese, A., Verity, J., Rebello, K., and Hof, R. (1996). The software revolution. *Business Week*, December 4, 75–90.

Cusumano, M. and Selby, R. (1995). *Microsoft Secrets.* NY: The Free Press.

Data Quest Corporation (1998, 1999, 2000, 2001).

Forbes (2001). The List: Fortune 500, *Forbes,* April 16, F3.

Fortune (2002). The list: Fortune 500, *Fortune,* April 15, F3.

France, M., Burrows, P., Himelstein, L., and Moeller, M. (1999). Does a break up make sense? *Business Week*, November 23, 38–42.

Gleick, J. (1995). Making Microsoft ok again. *The New York Times,* November 5, 50–64.

Gomes, L. (2000). Oracle, After a good year quintuples size of in-house venture capital fund. *Wall Street Journal,* B4.

Greene, J. (2000). The CZAR of the cyber-bazaar? *Business Week*, March 13, 34.

———. (2001). Microsoft: How it became stronger than ever. *Business Week*, June 4, 75–85.

Hamm, S., Cortese, A., and Burrows, P. (1998). No letup—and no apologies. *Business Week*, October 26, 58–64.

Harmon, A. (2001). Microsoft still faces a range of antitrust actions in US court. *New York Times*, June 29, C1.

Iwata, E. (1999). Oracle sees future as no. 1 software source on the net. *USA Today*, December 27, 4B.

Markoff, J. (2000). Windows 2000 facing a skeptical market. *New York Times*, February 14, B1.

Microsoft Corporation (2002). Microsoft financial facts. *www.Microsoft.com/ corporate info/fast fact.htm*

Moeller, M., Hamm, S., and Mullaney, T. J. (1999). Remaking Microsoft. *Business Week*, May 17, 106–114.

Nee, E. (1999). Microsoft gets ready to play a new game. *Fortune*, April 26, 107-112.

Pitta, J. (1999). Squeeze play: Databases get ugly. *Forbes,* February 22, 21–22.

Pollack, A. (1996). Nintendo-Microsoft deal on data delivery. *New York Times*, June 27.

Price, C. (2000). A certain success: But maybe slow in coming. *Financial Times*, February 16, 33.

Rebello, K. (1996). "Honey, What's on Microsoft?" *Business Week*, October 21, 134–136.

Schlender, B., and Kirkpatrick, D. (1995). The valley vs. Microsoft. *Fortune,* March 20, 84–90.

Schmidt, J. (1996). Microsoft network set to man the web. *USA Today*, April 24, B1.

Stewart, T. (1998). America's most advanced computer. *Fortune*, March 2, 71.

Wildstrom, S. (2000). Windows 2000: Worth the wait. *Business Week*, February 21, 20.

Wilke, J. (2000). Microsoft judge faces demand of market and monopoly law. *Wall Street Journal*, April 4, A1.

5

Best Practices of the Monsanto Company: Benchmarking World-Class Annual Reports

Ted J. Smith III and William C. Adams

As every investor knows, the coming of spring is marked not only by late snow storms and early-blooming flowers, but by the sudden efflorescence of another form of hardy perennial, the corporate annual report. Produced each year by over 11,000 publicly traded American companies at an estimated cost of more than $4 billion, and distributed in quantities numbering in the tens of millions, the annual report has become one of the most important and familiar products of corporate communication (Byrne 1987, 42; Zelvin 1987, 14; Flanagan 1993, 52). It must be noted, however, that its current prominence is a relatively recent phenomenon, the result a long period of evolution and refinement.

For the first quarter of the twentieth century, there were no formal disclosure requirements for American corporations. In 1926, however, the New York Stock Exchange began encouraging the companies it listed to make periodic reports to their investors. This initiative was followed by passage of the Securities Act of 1933 and the Securities and Exchange Act of 1934, which established formal requirements for publicly owned corporations to report to shareholders on a yearly basis financial information that could affect the value of the company. Some corporations and consultants were quick to recognize the marketing potential of these new annual reports (Droge, Germain, and Halstead 1990). But until about 1955 nearly all consisted of "little more than an income statement, a balance sheet, and a president's letter saying everything was wonderful" (Jacobson 1988, 52). Beginning in the mid-1950s, companies such as IBM, Litton, General Electric, and General Dynamics began to exploit the full communication and marketing potential of annual reports by introducing a range of innovations in form, content, and structure (Workman 1986).

By the mid-1980s, those innovations had become normative, at least in the reports issued by larger corporations ("Annual Report," 1984; Cato 1985, 19–20).

Among the most important and visible changes in form were the use of four-color printing, extensive photographs (first introduced in the 1940s) and informational graphics, imaginative design and layout, high-quality coated papers, varnished covers, and perfect binding (Workman 1986). In terms of content, the principal change was the addition of large amounts of optional unaudited information not required in the filings mandated by the Securities and Exchange Commission (SEC). In conjunction with the innovations in design and a series of expanded reporting requirements imposed by the SEC, the addition of this optional information not only increased the length of the average annual report to 40 pages or more but also encouraged adoption of the typical two-part structure that is now standard.

In this two-part structure, the report is divided into a narrative front section and a financial back section. The front section generally includes financial highlights, the president's letter to shareholders, and one or more narrative discussions or management interviews dealing with such topics as corporate performance and prospects, industry trends and competitive position, management philosophy and initiatives, corporate goals and strategies, product research and pipelines, marketing strategies, social and environmental commitments, and achievements and employee profiles. The back section consists principally of the required independent auditors' report, a series of mandatory financial statements, extensive notes to the financial statements, and a financial summary. In contrast to the audited and strictly regulated back section, material in the front section is unaudited and, except for the requirement that it must be consistent with the material in the back section, unregulated. The front section therefore offers an opportunity to present a much fuller image of the corporation and to address the interests and concerns of publics other than investors and the financial community, including employees, customers, opinion leaders, journalists, and activists. It was to exploit this opportunity that the innovations in form were introduced in the 1950s and their use has generally been restricted to the front section and covers of the report.

Preparation of the financial material now located in the back section of the report has always been the responsibility of corporate accountants and lawyers working in consultation with senior management, and it remains so today. But with the expansion and reformulation of the front section and efforts to "package" the report attractively, responsibility for preparing the front section and covers and for overseeing production of the report as a whole has been delegated increasingly to communication professionals. For example, a 1993 survey by the National Investor Relations Institute (NIRI) found that 42% of the companies surveyed gave responsibility for managing the annual report project to their investor relations department and another 36% to the corporate communications department ("The price of your annual checkup," 1993, 8).

Regardless of the locus of responsibility, it is clear that completion of the task requires a substantial commitment of time and resources. For example, a 1987 survey of 85 companies by consultant Sid Cato found that, on average, production of an annual report required 5.9 months of work by a team made up of a project manager (earning an annual salary of $53,470) and four assistants (as reported in Jacobson 1988, 53). Similarly, the 1993 NIRI survey found that 60% of large corporations (defined as those with annual revenues of $1 billion or more) budgeted at least $300,000 for their annual reports, and almost a third budgeted at least $400,000.

The question of whether these resources are well spent has been hotly contested for decades. Certainly annual reports are widely criticized, especially in the popular business press. For example, writers at *Business Week* have consistently adopted a quite cynical posture in that publication's yearly overview article on annual reports, as the titles of several recent offerings suggest: "This Year's Annual Reports: Show Business as Usual" (Byrne 1987, 42); "And Now, from Fantasyland   It's Annual Report Time" (Rothman and Fins 1990, 32); "It's Corporate America's Spring Hornblowing Festival" (Kang 1993, 31). Also common are articles which focus on real or alleged instances of mendacity (for example, Hector 1989; "Putting a Happy Face," 1990) or offer advice on how to avoid being misled by them (for example, Weiss 1987; Dunn 1988).

At a somewhat more reflective level, critics have tended to ground their case in three interrelated claims (see for example Girdler 1963; Jacobson 1988, 52): few people bother to read annual reports, and those who do find that they lack credibility and are of little use in making investment decisions. Although more often asserted than argued, these claims are sometimes supported by selected research results, especially the findings of a series of surveys commissioned by Hill and Knowlton in the mid-1980s (see "Annual Report," 1984,

1987) and widely cited by commentators thereafter. In particular, nearly half of the 247 individual investors interviewed in a 1984 survey reported that they either ignore (4.9%) or merely skim (42.5%) the annual reports they receive. The same study found that 73% of the individual investors agreed with the statement, "Annual reports often play down bad news or hide it in the back of the report" and that 46 of the 50 professional investors surveyed agreed that "Annual reports all too often fail to candidly discuss bad news, problems and what management is doing about them" ("Annual Report," 1984, 31). Similarly, a 1986 survey of 501 shareholders and 50 security analysts found large majorities of both groups agreeing with the statement, "Annual reports don't tell the whole story. They play down the negatives and only report management's viewpoint" ("Do Annual Reports Count?" 1987, 12). Finally, and perhaps most important, the Hill and Knowlton surveys have consistently reported that individual investors put little faith in annual reports as information sources. For example, in the 1986 survey ("Do Annual Reports Count?" 1987, 12), only 3% of the shareholders said annual reports are where they get "the best investment information," well behind newspapers (35%), business periodicals (19%), stockbrokers (18%), statistical services (4%), and even friends and relatives (4%).

Although criticisms of annual reports are common, the fact is that most published comments are favorable, often stressing their unique and uniquely important communication functions. In the view of consultant Elizabeth Howard (1991, 26), "The annual report is a company's primary calling card; the lasting visual impression of a company." Deborah Kelly, then vice president of corporate affairs for Quaker Oats, told a panel organized by *Financial Executive* magazine, "The annual report is often the only opportunity the company has to tell people what they're going to do. We use it for that purpose, and we consider it a very important marketing function ("The Annual Report," 1985, 34)." According to Richard Lewis, chairman and CEO of Corporate Annual Reports, Inc. (1987, 21), "[T]he annual report is widely accepted as a company's most credible and comprehensive document." David Haggie, managing director of the British firm Annual Reports, Ltd., makes the case in somewhat greater detail (1984, 66):

> How, therefore, can a company communicate with its environment? Advertising, public relations and corporate design are all methods of communication. The annual report, however, is special. It contains all of these elements and more. It is a statutory document which is given credibility by its very nature.

The auditor's report gives it stature. The chairman's report reflects his personality. The review of the business and directors' report reflect the company's personality. Therefore the annual report is the prime medium for projecting a company at its audience.

While it should be noted that many of the strongest proponents of annual reports are those in the business of writing them, they are able to array a substantial amount of research to support their views and rebut the claims of their critics. In particular, proponents can argue that the question of how carefully annual reports are read depends largely on how one chooses to interpret the available evidence. For example, while it is true that nearly half of the individual investors in the 1984 Hill and Knowlton survey reported that they ignored or merely skimmed the annual reports they received, it is also true that the same survey found that a majority of those investors reported that they either read (32.8%) or studied (18.2%) them ("Annual Report," 1984, 32). Further, all of the relevant research shows that financial analysts and institutional investors read the reports they receive with great care. As far as credibility is concerned, proponents will generally concede that annual reports are widely perceived as tendentious and sometimes less than candid (see for example the discussion in "Annual Report: Part One," 1985), but they can also point to a large body of survey evidence which shows that annual reports are typically rated as the principal source of investment information by all of the major investor groups (see especially Bishop 1975; Most and Chang 1979; Chang, Most, and Brain, 1983; Epstein and Pava 1993, 1994a, 1994b; Hutchins 1994; Fulkerson 1996). For example, in their massive three-nation survey of 4,000 individual investors, 900 institutional investors, and 900 financial analysts, Chang, Most, and Brain (1983) found that all three American groups rated corporate annual reports as their most important source of information for investment decisions. These and many similar findings directly contradict the widely cited results of the Hill and Knowlton surveys, which appear to be artifactual.

It seems likely that the conflict between critics and proponents of annual reports will continue indefinitely. At the practical level, however, there appears to be widespread consensus on three points. First, annual reports will continue to be widely used for the foreseeable future, either in their traditional form or in the form of the simplified summary annual report introduced with great fanfare by the McKesson Corporation in 1987 (for example, Simone 1988) and still the subject of extensive discussion (for example, Cook and Sutton,

1995). Second, while there is disagreement about the actual effectiveness of annual reports, few question their potential for being a valuable corporate communications tool. Third, and perhaps most important, even those who doubt the positive potential of annual reports will generally concede that a poorly designed report can have a substantial negative impact on the way a corporation is perceived.

Given these realities, the question of how to produce an effective annual report is one of substantial importance for corporate communication practitioners. Unfortunately, neither the relevant research literature nor the practical literature on annual reports offers them much usable guidance. In the research literature, the most valuable studies are those based on surveys of the various major audiences of annual reports. In addition to the global measures of usage and satisfaction noted above, these studies provide evidence about the specific kinds of information accessed and desired in the reports (for example, Bishop 1975; Epstein and Pava 1994a; 1995) and the reactions of readers to innovations such as summary annual reports (for example, Hutchins, 1994; Epstein and Pava, 1994b). Also valuable in this regard are the findings of a small number of observational studies of the way annual reports are actually used by their recipients in the financial community (for example, Day 1986; Gniewosz 1990).

A second and larger group of studies focuses on the content of annual reports. The simplest of these merely analyze and evaluate selected features such as readability (Hoskins 1984; Heath and Phelps 1984; Courtis 1987; Schroeder and Gibson 1990), depiction of women (Newsom 1988; Anderson and Imperia 1992), expression of customer commitment (Judd and Tims 1991), use of graphs (Beattie and Jones 1992), predictive accuracy (Fisher and Hu 1988/89; Pava and Epstein 1993) and information provided in the management discussion and analysis section (Collins, Davie, and Weetman 1993). Typically, their evaluative conclusions are derived from the application of some theoretical ideal; in those few instances where the effects of variations in the feature of interest are reported (Means 1981, on readability; Kuiper 1988, on depiction of women), the findings suggest that the features have little impact. Other studies have examined the relationship between selected content features such as the themes (Ingram and Frazier 1983; McConnell, Haslem, and Gibson 1986; Swales 1988; Kohut and Segars 1992), readability (Courtis 1986; Subramanian, Insley, and Blackwell 1993; Jones 1994) and causal reasoning patterns (Bettman and Weitz 1983; Salancik and Meindl 1984; Clapham and Schwenk 1991) of the president's letter and various measures of performance. Although not devoid of practical implications for those tasked with producing annual reports, these findings are perhaps more useful to financial analysts. Finally, a small number of studies provide fragmentary evidence of the impact of selected features of annual reports on financial markets and investor decisions.

The most useful findings are that inclusion of nonearnings data (Ou 1990) and use of self-serving attributions (Staw, McKechnie, and Puffer 1983) are both associated with increases in stock prices, and that financial analysts (Bell 1984) may place greater weight on data presented in nonnumerical form in those cases where accepted numerical performance measures are unavailable (for example, in evaluating R&D companies).

In addition to the rather modest research literature on annual reports, there is a continuous flow of more pragmatic articles in a wide range of business and business communication publications. Nearly all of these can be placed into one of three general categories: descriptive, evaluative or prescriptive. Descriptive articles (e.g., Dunk 1980; Badaracco 1988; Poe 1994) generally combine a discussion of current trends in the form and content of annual reports with speculation about impending developments. Evaluative articles—by far the largest group—either criticize specific reports or practices or present the winners of the various yearly contests for the best (and sometimes worst) reports (e.g., Cato 1999, 2000; Lowengard 1996; "Print's Annual Report," 1996). Finally, the prescriptive articles offer either arguments on the need for some innovation or practical advice on how to produce an annual report (e.g., Moldenhauer 1983; Denmarsh and Esteban 1988; Millman 1990; de Haan, 1996).

Despite the large number of these articles, they provide relatively little reliable guidance for the communication practitioner. The principal reason for this is that the insights and recommendations they offer lack any validation beyond common sense and the testimony of experts. In particular, there is almost no documentary evidence reported in either the research or the practical literature on what practices are effective in accomplishing the marketing and communication functions of annual reports. And the experts, as usual, tend to be divided in their opinions, with the result that their claims are often incompatible and sometimes contradictory. Of course, the evaluative articles do provide a number of positive (and negative) exemplars. But aside from the problem that these are the product of subjective judgments based on criteria which are often criticized as arbitrary (see, for example, Galant 1988, 70), the very fact that they are examples makes it difficult to generalize their features to different circumstances. In contrast, the prescriptive articles do offer advice in the form of general principles. But with a few notable exceptions (see especially Foy 1973; Lewis 1987; and Marino 1995), these principles are so basic and so general (for example, "Maintain an audience orientation," or "Tie the report to corporate objectives," both from Denmarsh and Esteban 1988, 35) that they function as little more than theoretical guidelines. What is missing is any method for translating them into practice and validating the results.

In order to address these deficiencies, the remainder of this chapter will apply the technique of benchmarking to the problem of producing effective annual reports. It will begin by describing the development of a simple, research-based method for designing the form and content of annual reports and validating their effectiveness. It will then list a number of practical insights derived from several years of using this method to produce a series of award-winning annual reports. The method offered here as a benchmark was developed by the Monsanto Company, a Fortune 500 Corporation headquartered in suburban St. Louis, Missouri, working in conjunction with Adams Research, Inc., a communications research and consulting firm located in Arlington, Virginia (now operating as Market and Communications Research, Inc., in Rockville, Maryland).

The Monsanto Method

Development of what might be called the Monsanto method began in 1990, when Scarlett Foster, who went on to become corporate director of public affairs, was assigned the task of producing the company's 1990 annual report. Throughout her career, Foster had stressed the importance of using the findings of systematic, carefully interpreted research to inform decision making in corporate communications. For example, as a community relations specialist for one of Monsanto's manufacturing plants, she collaborated in initiating one of the company's first community surveys to measure how residents viewed the plant. She then used the findings to build an informed community relations plan and tracked its progress with subsequent surveys. Later put in charge of corporate financial communications, Foster worked with an outside research firm to design a quarterly media content analysis to systematically track the tone, themes, and trends of Monsanto's coverage. And when Monsanto embarked on a major round of corporate restructuring, she inaugurated periodic e-mail surveys to evaluate the success of efforts to explain the new steps to employees (91% of whom were online) and to measure their morale.

The challenge Foster faced in 1990 was substantial. At the time, Monsanto consisted of five very different operating units which specialized in the diverse areas of pharmaceuticals (Searle), sweeteners (NutraSweet), precision manufacturing (Fisher Controls), agricultural products (the Agricultural Group), and chemicals (the Chemical Group). The most obvious problem was to find a way to clearly and succinctly explain Monsanto's complex technical, medical, and scientific activities. To make matters worse, however, many of its products, especially those of the Chemical Group, are intermediary products which are sold to other companies and are several steps removed from any easily explained consumer end use. Finally, 1990 was not proving to be a particularly good year for the company financially. Altogether, it was not an easy task.

What is distinctive about Foster's response is that she began immediately to investigate ways to use research to inform the task. This led her to conclude that the report could best be improved by obtaining systematic feedback from its principal audiences. In October of 1990, she contacted Bill Adams, a researcher with whom she had worked on the projects mentioned above, to explore the possibility of using focus groups for that purpose. One part of her proposal—evaluating the effectiveness of the final published report by submitting it to focus groups in the spring—was rarely done at the time but not unheard of. The second part, however, was more innovative. Here the idea was to obtain focus group reactions to key portions of the draft text in the late fall while the full report was still being written. In order to avoid any SEC early disclosure violations, the tested material (including the covers, front section, and some collateral nonfinancial material from the back section) would have to be masked by inserting fictional company and product names and by omitting or changing any financial data.

In theory, at least, the proposal seemed sound. Focus groups can be used to explore reactions to any stimulus—oral, written, visual or artifactual—but they are ideally suited for message testing. One advantage is that they can elicit from the participants a large body of highly detailed and subtly nuanced responses to the message as a whole or any of its parts. In the hands of a skilled facilitator, they also offer the flexibility to fully explore unanticipated issues and insights as they arise in the course of the discussion. Finally, by using the Directed Feedback Method, in which participants complete portions of a survey questionnaire after each discussion segment, it is possible to obtain precise, quantitative data from the group as a whole and, if desired, to track changes in the group's perceptions over time. Of course, because focus groups are based on small and selected samples, care must be taken in generalizing their findings to any larger population. But the great strength of focus groups is that they provide the opportunity to explore the dynamics of why certain communications are effective and why others fail. Such lessons provide insights that extend beyond the narrow specifics under study and can be used to generate broader, cumulative principles to inform future efforts.

In this situation, however, there was considerable doubt whether focus groups could be used successfully. One concern was that the mock annual report might not be taken seriously by the participants. Another was whether there would be enough similarity in their responses to provide any useful guidance. This was especially problematic because Foster wanted to conduct two separate focus groups, one of securities analysts and the other of individual investors. Both groups were obviously important target audiences for the report. Moreover, the conventional wisdom was that the two groups took widely different approaches to evaluating annual reports. So it seemed important to test the text with both. But if the conventional wisdom was right, there was a very real chance that the groups would produce contradictory findings.

Despite these concerns, the decision was made to proceed with the focus groups. But partly as a hedge against failure, Foster also commissioned two academic specialists with extensive experience in public relations (Ted J. Smith and Debra Dean, who also served as the focus group facilitator) to prepare independent critiques of the draft annual report. Their findings, based on a detailed analysis of design and graphics and a word-by-word evaluation of the text, could then be used to supplement the more global responses of the focus group participants.

In November of 1990, Adams assembled two focus groups in Montgomery County, Maryland, an affluent suburb of Washington, D.C. One was made up of a dozen serious investors, most of whom had securities portfolios in excess of $100,000, who said they look at annual reports. The second included a similar number of securities analysts who had been recruited from the published membership list of the Washington Society of Investment Analysts. About two-thirds of them listed pharmaceutical and chemical companies among the fields they followed closely.

The results of the focus group sessions surpassed even the most optimistic expectations. None of the anticipated problems materialized and a number of significant insights were recorded. Among the most important findings (all of which have been confirmed in subsequent research for Monsanto and other companies):

- Readers started from a far lower knowledge base than had been suspected. The text took too much for granted and assumed far more familiarity with the industry, the company, and its products than was justified. Terms and products needed simple, basic explanations.

- Readers rejected as superfluous some of the human interest material that Foster and her team had prepared to feature in the front portion of the report. For example, they did not care about the interesting background of the new head of the company's Brazilian operations. Some could tolerate it as a small sidebar, but others were annoyed to see anything that distracted them from their sole mission: to size up the company's merits as an investment.

- To a surprising degree, neither analysts nor investors cared much about the events of the past. Although an annual report is ostensibly a retrospective look at the preceding year, these readers were not acting as historians, but as futurists. They really wanted to discover where the company was headed, its plans and strategies, its leaders' direction, its products' chances for success. Furthermore, they did not want to have to guess those things; they wanted the report to focus explicitly on the future.

- In this vein, readers were unexpectedly forgiving when it came to past mistakes. In their view, what mattered was where the company went from there. They even criticized the company for being too apologetic for a past shortcoming. In their eyes, the market had already delivered its punishment and the suitable sentence had already been served.

- The focus groups also proved valuable in uncovering little "snags" in the text, those sentences or phrases which, for some unanticipated reason, distract, confuse, or disturb readers. Thus irritated, the reader shifts into a less sympathetic and more argumentative stance. The focus group sessions turned out to be opportune vehicles for catching such small, but highly damaging, problems.

In retrospect, it is now clear why focus groups proved to be such a valuable tool. The annual report is produced by a relatively small group of insiders who are themselves highly familiar with their company's saga. That these people are so close to their subject is unavoidable and inescapable. But that proximity is a disadvantage as well as an advantage. The major strength of the focus group is that it opens up the process to in-depth feedback. The creators can thus see their product through the fresh eyes of their actual audiences.

Given the remarkable success of the first round of focus groups, the process was repeated in the spring of 1991 to test reactions to Monsanto's published 1990 report. As in the fall, the first group was made up of affluent Maryland investors. But the second session was held in New York and drew its participants from the ranks of sophisticated Wall Street analysts. This "post-test" also proved to be an instructive exercise. In addition to generating feedback on how well the problems identified in the fall had been resolved, it provided evidence of the effectiveness of the final report and suggested new possibilities for the future. In particular, use of the finished report allowed participants to offer valuable criticisms about its design and layout.

The spring focus groups also offered a chance to study how analysts and investors "digest" an annual report. They revealed that the investors focused overwhelmingly on the front section and wanted very basic information about the company and its products. In contrast, the securities analysts looked closely at the entire report (not just the financial data in the back, as some investor relations experts had claimed) to gain insights into management thinking, to see what image management wanted to convey, to look at the financial data, and to check for consistency with other sources. Another surprising finding was that, despite differences in the way they use a report, the ultimate opinions of the analysts and the investors were usually quite similar. To a remarkable extent, they reached the same conclusions about things as varied as the appeal of the cover, the merits of the chairman's letter, and whether the tone of the report was too optimistic or too defensive.

With one small refinement (a reduction in the number of detailed critiques from two to one), the Monsanto method has taken the same form since it was first developed in 1990–91: investor and analyst focus groups and a detailed critique of the draft annual report in the fall, followed by two similar focus groups to evaluate the published report in the spring. By at least one measure, the method met immediately with considerable success. In just the six years from 1990 through 1995, Monsanto's reports received 15 major awards of excellence from four different groups, including *Institutional Investor* magazine (1990, 1992, 1993, 1994), the International Association of Business Communicators (1991, 1993, 1995), the National Association of Investors Corporation (1991, 1993, 1994, 1995) and *Financial World* magazine (1992, 1993, 1994, 1995). Obviously, focus group research is not the only reason why Scarlett Foster and her team have earned such widespread recognition. But she has stressed its value for annual reports in addresses to groups such as the St. Louis Public Relations Society and the Annual Conference on Annual Reports. It should also be noted that a number of other corporations have worked with Adams Research to use the Monsanto method in preparing their annual reports, and all have received national recognition for their efforts. In fact, nearly every annual report known to have been produced by this method has been ranked among Sid Cato's top 20 annual reports of the year.

Practical Insights

Over the years, Adams Research has identified a number recurring elements in the way analysts and investors approach annual reports. The most recent focus groups have continued to reconfirm the validity of these general findings:

- Annual reports address two distinct audiences: (1) Investors who focus on the front section and want basic information about the company and its products; and (2) financial analysts who read both sections to obtain financial data, to check for consistency with other data sources, to see what image management wants to convey, and to gain insights into management thinking.

- Both analysts and investors are mainly concerned with the following:

  1. Profitability (for the future more than the past)

  2. Future direction and leadership (company goals and how its leaders intend to get there)

  3. Current and future products (the present money-making products and those in the pipeline with a promising future)

- All three of these concerns are directed toward a company's future performance. Historical data are of interest only to the extent that they offer clues about future success.

- Annual reports are seen as public relations efforts. Thus, readers approach reports with great skepticism and are extremely sensitive to wording, omissions, and any perceived discrepancies. They expect the company to put its best foot forward. If no negatives are mentioned, they suspect a cover-up. Yet, any problem that is mentioned is likely to be magnified in the reader's mind as perhaps even more severe than the company admits. Despite their skepticism, however, analysts and investors still see the annual report as an important reflection of the company. A report can inspire confidence or create doubts.

- Annual reports are frequently skimmed rather than studied. Readers are impatient. They want to be able to extract the key messages quickly and easily from the text. Consequently, they like layered presentations, replete with bullet points, bold highlights, call-outs, and other such devices.

- Satisfaction with an annual report is closely related to comprehension. Readers who do not understand a report quickly become annoyed. If the document is difficult to understand, the individual investor is likely to toss it aside. Readers want to see technical terms explained. Graphics, format, charts, photographs, and captions are also powerful tools to improve comprehension, not just to make the publication look attractive.

- Comprehension of the report (and thus satisfaction with it) are greatly enhanced when key themes are emphasized throughout the report. "Repetition with variation" is the classic tool of effective communications and is especially necessary for written material that tends to be skimmed rather than studied. At the same time, too much overt repetition can sometimes bother those important readers who do closely review the report.

- As noted above, most readers know far less about the company than the authors of annual reports may suppose. Writers often make the mistake of assuming too much background knowledge on the part of the audience. Investors often want the most elementary information about the company. Analysts unfamiliar with the company may also find this information useful.

- Annual reports are interpreted as reflecting the judgment of top management. The tone of the entire report, not just the chairman's letter, is thought to reveal much about the attitude and mindset of the company's leaders. Likewise, both investors and analysts say they are repelled by an ostentatious annual report. They want the reports to be attractive but not lavish.

Adams Research has also identified numerous specific content and structural features which enhance the effectiveness of annual reports. Many were first noted in a study of award-winning annual reports commissioned by Monsanto in 1991. All have since been validated by focus group research across a number of corporations and industries. Among the most important are the following:

- The best annual reports present a unified whole in which every item of information serves a specific function. This is usually accomplished by building the report around a single theme. The most effective themes share two important characteristics: (1) More than just a slogan, the theme is linked to key performance data and is an integral part of the argumentative structure of the report; and (2) all elements of the report are used to express the theme: text, financial data, graphs, covers, photos, and captions.

- Nearly all annual reports emphasize the same general goals and commitments: excellence, growth, adaptive change, service, quality, innovation, building on strengths, strategic planning, effective and enlightened management, the paramount importance of customers and shareholders, maximizing earnings, empowerment of skilled and dedicated employees, effective competition in an era of global interdependence, and social responsibility. In order to make these commitments credible, they should be supported by detailed and specific information about the company's actions.

- Negative information is best addressed through candid but optimistic discussion. Merely acknowledging the existence of a problem, however, serves little positive purpose. Effective candor requires that acknowledgment of a problem be followed immediately with a discussion of its nature and solution.

- Nearly every company claims to have a strategic plan that will allow it to achieve its objectives. To a significant degree, investment in a company is a product of confidence in this plan and the managers who will implement it. Confidence can be enhanced by candid explanations of earlier failures and of potential obstacles that could require a change in the plan. An additional advantage of the latter course is that it provides reasonable grounds for explaining failures in the future while preserving the credibility of the managers who foresaw them.

- Just as there are different possible criteria for judging an annual report, there are different possible criteria for judging corporate performance. A report can therefore influence evaluations by proposing its own criteria for judgment.

- In a genre where hyperbole is the norm, precise but understated characterizations can have great impact.

- In structuring a report, the front cover can be used quite effectively to focus attention on a content theme. But the content should be sufficiently rich to merit close attention.

- There are strong conventions about the kinds of information—especially financial highlights—that should appear at the very beginning of a report. Use of that space for other material disorients the reader.

- The major points in a report should be ordered deductively, that is, from general to specific. This facilitates skimming, allows for useful repetition, and is presupposed by the standard format of annual reports. Among other problems, information presented inductively (leading from specific data to a more general conclusion) is ineffective if the reader does not read through to the end.

- Because readers process information sequentially, information is best structured as a single coherent flow. The greater the number of different flows of information on a page (as developed in the text, boxes, photos, captions, graphs, and tables), the greater the probability that some will be skipped.

- While explanatory information such as definitions of basic financial terms is useful for the novice, it is of little value for the knowledgeable reader. Whenever possible, therefore, it should be located outside the main flow of the text.

- An interview can be a more effective and efficient method of conveying complex information than an essay. It eliminates the need for transitional material and, because the questions serve as headings, it facilitates skimming.

- Bar, line, and pie graphs are now a standard feature of annual reports. Although they do have decorative aspects, their principal purpose is to provide a clear, succinct, and accurate visual representation of quantified information. In general, the most effective graphs use bright colors and a simple, traditional format. Innovative graphs are almost invariably based on some distortion of a spatial dimension. Whatever their artistic merits, these distortions almost always make it more difficult for the reader to decipher the graph and therefore seriously undermine their principal purpose.

There is no question that the preparation of an annual report will always be more of an applied art than an exact science. But it is also evident that carefully designed and interpreted research can assist the process by providing guidance in the form of both useful principles and highly specific feedback. It is for that reason that the Monsanto method merits inclusion in any discussion of best practices in corporate communication.

References

Anderson, C. J., and Imperia, G. (1992). The corporate annual report: A photo analysis of male and female portrayals. *The Journal of Business Communication*, 29 (2): 113–28.

Annual report credibility (1984). *Public Relations Journal*, (November): 31–34.

The annual report, part one: Is it filling its role? (1985). *Financial Executive*, November, 30–35.

Badaracco, C. (1988). Smoke and substance: Trends in annual reports. *Public Relations Quarterly*, 33(1):13–17.

Beattie, V., and Jones, M. J. (1992). The use and abuse of graphs in annual reports: Theoretical framework and empirical study. *Accounting and Business Research*, 291–303.

Bell, J. (1984). The effect of presentation form on the use of information in annual reports. *Management Science* 30(2):169–85.

Bettman, J. R., and Weitz, B. A. (1983). Attributions in the board room: Causal reasoning in corporate annual reports. *Administrative Science Quarterly* 28:165–83.

Bishop, S. A. (1975). What investors want to know. *Public Relations Journal*, September, 36–37.

Byrne, J. A. (1987). This year's annual reports: Show business as usual. *Business Week*, April 13, 42.

Cato, S. (1985). The annual report: "Here I come world." *Public Relations Quarterly* 30(1):17–21.

———. (1999). The 10 best and 10 worst annual reports of 1998. *Chief Executive*, November, 48–56, 58.

———. (2000). Getting better all the time. *Chief Executive*, November, 42–47.

Chang, L. S., Most, K. S., and Brain, C. W. (1983). The utility of annual reports: An international study. *Journal of International Business Studies* (Spring/Summer): 63–84.

Clapham, S. E., and Schwenk, C. R. (1991). Self-serving attributions, managerial cognition and company performance. *Strategic Management Journal* 12:219–29.

Collins, W., Davie, E. S., and Weetmam, P. (1993). Management discussion and analysis: An evaluation of practice in US and UK companies. *Accounting and Business Research* 23(90):123–37.

Cook, J. M., and Sutton, M. H. (1995). Summary annual reporting: A cure for information overload. *Financial Executive*, January–February, 12–15.

Courtis, J. K. (1986). An investigation into annual report readability and corporate risk-return relationships. *Accounting and Business Research*, autumn, 285–94.

———. (1987). Fry, smog, lix and rix: Insinuations about corporate business communications. *The Journal of Business Communication* 24(2):19–27.

Day, J. F. S. (1986). The use of annual reports by UK investment analysts. *Accounting and Business Research*, autumn, 295–307.

Denmarsh, R. I., and Esteban, F. R. (1988). How to produce a credible annual report. *Public Relations Journal* (October): 35–36.

Droge, C., Germain, R., and Halstead, D. (1990). A note on marketing and the corporate annual report: 1930–1950. *Journal of the Academy of Marketing Science*, 18(4):355–64.

Dunk, W. P. (August 1980). 28 trends in annual reports. *Public Relations Journal* (August): 10–13.

Dunn, J. (July 1988). Facts from figures. *Accountancy*, July, 131–32.

Epstein, M. J., and Pava, M. L. (1993). *The Shareholders' Use of Corporate Annual Reports*. Greenwich, Conn.: JAI Press, 1993.

————. (1994a). Profile of an annual report. *Financial Executive*, January–February, 41–43.

————. (1994b). Individual investors' perceptions of the summary annual report: A survey approach. *Journal of Applied Business Research* 10(3):60–67.

————. (1995). Shareholders' perceptions of the usefulness of MD&As. *Managerial Finance*, 21(3):68–83.

Fisher, S. A., and Yu, M. Y. (1988/89). Does the CEO's letter to the shareholders have predictive validity? *Business Forum*, fall/winter, 22–24.

Flanagan, P. (1993). Make your annual report work harder. *Management Review*, October, 52–58.

Foy, F. C. (1973). Annual reports don't have to be dull. *Harvard Business Review*, January–February, 49–58.

Fulkerson, J. (1996). How investors use annual reports. *American Demographics* 18(5):16–19.

Galant, D. (1988). The wacky world of Sid Cato. *Institutional Investor*, July, 67–70.

Girdler, R. (1963). 18,000,000 books nobody reads. *Saturday Review*, April 13, 71.

Gniewosz, G. (1990). The share investment decision process and information use: An exploratory case study. *Accounting and Business Research* (summer): 223–30.

de Haan, C. (1996). Have a good year: 10 golden rules for annual reports. *Director*, May, 34.

Do annual reports count? (1987). *Public Relations Journal* (February): 12.

Haggie, D. (1984). The annual report as an aid to communication. *Accountancy*, August, 66–69.

Heath, R. L., and Phelps, G. (1984). Annual reports II: Readability of reports vs. business press. *Public Relations Review* 10(2):56–62.

Hector, G. (1989). Cute tricks on the bottom line. *Fortune*, April 24, 193–200.

Hoskins, R. L. (1984). Annual reports I: Difficult reading and getting more so. *Public Relations Review*, 10(2):49–55.

Howard, E. (1991). Preparing annual reports in the 1990s. *Public Relations Journal* (May): 26–27.

Hutchins, H. R. (1994). Annual reports: Earning surprising respect from institutional investors. *Public Relations Review* 20(4):309–17.

Ingram, R. W., and Frazier, K. B. (1983). Narrative disclosures in annual reports. *Journal of Business Research* 11:49–60.

Jacobson, G. (1988). How valuable is the annual report? *Management Review* (October): 51–53.

Jones, M. J. (1994). A comment to contextualize "Performance and readability: A comparison of annual reports of profitable and unprofitable companies." *The Journal of Business Communication* 31(3):225–33.

Judd, V. C., and Tims, B. J. (1991). How annual reports communicate a customer orientation. *Industrial Marketing Management* 20:353–60.

Kang, G. M. (1993). It's corporate America's spring hornblowing festival. *Business Week*, April 12, 31.

Kohut, G. F., and Segars, A. H. (1992). The president's letter to stockholders: An examination of corporate communication strategy. *The Journal of Business Communication*, 29(1):7–21.

Kuiper, S. (1988). Gender representation in corporate annual reports and perceptions of corporate climate. *The Journal of Business Communication*, 25(3):87–94.

Lewis, R. A. (1987). The annual report: A tool to achieve the CEO's objectives. *Directors and Boards*, 11(3):19–23.

Lowengard, M. (1996). Annual reports 1995. *Institutional Investor*, September, 105–10.

Marino, A. J., Jr. (1995). Separating your annual report from the herd. *Public Relations Quarterly* 40(2):44–47.

McConnell, D., Haslem, J. A., and Gibson, V. R. (1986). The president's letter to stockholders: A new look. *Financial Analysts Journal*, (September–October): 66–70.

Means, T. L. (1981). Readability: An evaluative criterion of stockholder reaction to annual reports. *The Journal of Business Communication*, 18(1):25–33.

Millman, R. B. (1990). Making the most of your annual report. *Management Review*, October, 52–55.

Moldenhauer, C. A. (1983). Begin with the basics. *Public Relations Journal* (November): 42–43.

Most, K. S., and Chang, L. S. (1979). How useful are annual reports to investors? *The Journal of Accountancy* (September): 111–13.

Newsom, D. (1988). How women are depicted in annual reports. *Public Relations Review*, 14(3):15–19.

Ou, J. A. (1990). The information content of nonearnings accounting numbers as earnings predictors. *Journal of Accounting Research*, 28(1):144–63.

Pava, M. L., and Epstein, M. J. (1993). How good is MD&A as an investment tool? *Journal of Accountancy* (March): 51–53.

Poe, R. (1994). Can we talk? *Across the Board*, May, 17–23.

The price of your annual checkup. (1993). *Financial Executive,* July/August, 8.

Print's annual report on annual reports (1996). *Print*, March–April, 74–81.

Putting a happy face on the awful truth (1990). *Business Month*, June, 25.

Rothman, A., and Fins, A. (1990). And now, from fantasyland . . . It's annual report time. *Business Week*, April 30, 32.

Salancik, G. R., and Meindl, J. R. (1984). Corporate attributions as strategic illusions of management control. *Administrative Science Quarterly*, 29:238–54.

Schroeder, N., and Gibson, C. (1990). Readability of management's discussion and analysis. *Accounting Horizons*, December, 78–87.

Simone, T. B. (1988). Behind the scenes: How McKesson produced the first summary annual report. *Financial Executive*, January–February, 49–52.

Staw, B. M., McKechnie, P. I., and Puffer, S. M. (1983). The justification of organizational performance. *Administrative Science Quarterly* 28:582–600.

Subramanian, R., Insley, R. G., and Blackwell, R. D. (1993). Performance and readability: A comparison of annual reports of profitable and unprofitable corporations. *The Journal of Business Communication* 30(1):49–61.

Swales, G. S., Jr. (1988). Another look at the president's letter to stockholders. *Financial Analysts Journal* (March–April): 71–73.

Weiss, G. (1987). Reading between the lines of an annual report. *Business Week*, March 23, 164–65.

Workman, J. A. (1986). Annual reports: Going from the boardroom to your livingroom. *Graphic Arts Monthly*, June, 82–84.

Zelvin, A. (1987). Your annual report is an award-winner. You're fired. *Industry Week*, September 7, 14.

Part 2

Limiting Factors in Implementing Best Practices

Ernest and Young reported the results of a five-year study of over 500 firms on quality control. They conclude that only top performing firms have the internal skills, financial resources, and know-how to successfully benchmark the world's best firms.

(Obloj, Cushman, and Kozminski, 1995:120)

In **Part 2** we explore and illustrate three major limiting factors to implementing the benchmarking of organizational best practices:

1. *organizational learning capabilities* as a limiting factor in IBM's PC unit's attempt to implement the benchmarking of the Dell Computer firm's best practices;

2. *time* as a limiting factor in the Danville Bumper Works's attempt to implement the benchmarking of the Toyota Motor corporation's best practices; and

3. *corporate culture* as a limiting factor in ABB's attempt to implement the benchmarking of the General Electric Corporation's best practices.

6

Organizational Learning as a Limiting Factor: A Case Study of IBM's PC Unit

The Japanese word dantotsy *means striving to be the best of the best. It captures the essence of benchmarking, which is a positive, proactive process designed to change operations in a structured fashion to achieve superior performance. The purpose of benchmarking is to increase the probability of success of an attempt to gain a competitive advantage.*

(Camp, 1992.3)

In a provocative five-year study of 500 multinational organizations, the Ernst and Young consulting group suggested that most of the firms they studied lacked the organizational learning capabilities to engage in the benchmarking of world-class performance. Even more provocative was the study's conclusion that an organization or unit of an organization's success or failure in benchmarking was readily predicted by its value added per employee (VAE) and its return on assets (ROA) prior to attempting to implement bench marked best practices. Ernst and Young then classified an organization or unit of an organization as Novice, Journeyman, or Master based upon its performance on these two measures. Only those firms classified as Masters with a VAE of $74,000+ per employee or an ROA of 7 percent or more were capable of learning sufficiently well from a world-class performance to successfully benchmark and put in place a similar operation in their own firm or unit (Port et al. 1992, 66–67).

Consider the case of IBM, which between 1986 and 1992 had vaporized $60 billion in stockholder value, taken a $17 billion charge against profits to reengineer, laid off 100,000 workers, and watched its sales and market shares across its five major markets shrink (Sherman 1994, 82). In mid-April of 1993, Lou Gerstner was brought in from outside IBM as CEO to lead IBM's turnaround. Gerstner began the turnaround by taking a $8.9 billion charge against earnings, selling

$26 billion in buildings and property, and saving $8 billion in overhead by downsizing. By April 1995, IBM had returned to profitability in most of its businesses. However, IBM's PC unit was still losing money. Jerome York, IBM's CFO, said it was unclear when the PC unit would turn around (Hays 1995, B6). Three years later IBM's PC unit would benchmark the world-class performance of Dell Computer Corporation in an attempt to improve its own profitability. IBM's PC unit thus offers a unique opportunity to test Ernst and Young's claims regarding VAE and ROA.

It will be the purpose of our case study to explore Ernst and Young's claim regarding the need to have a $74,000+ VAE or a 7 percent ROA to be capable of successfully benchmarking a world-class performance. By 1998, several IBM businesses would meet these Master criteria in VAE and ROA, but IBM's PC unit's performance would not meet the same criteria. Our task divides itself into three parts: (1) a summary of IBM's PC unit's performance between 1994 and 1997, (2) a summary of IBM's benchmarking of Dell in 1998 and its effectiveness in implementing that benchmarking, and (3) conclusions regarding the legitimacy of Ernst and Young's claim regarding the learning capabilities of organizations as a limiting factor in world-class benchmarking.

IBM's PC Unit's Performance from 1994 to 1997

IBM's Chairman Louis Gerstner has long maintained that the home PC market is a "growth opportunity that we cannot and will not ignore." With only 40% of U.S. households and 15% of global households owning a computer, it is an attractive market for a world-wide company like IBM.

(Narisetti, 1997:B1)

In 1994, Gerstner brought in a new top executive, Richard Thoman, from outside the computer industry to head IBM's PC unit. Thoman was immediately confronted with a series of problems. First, there was a $700 million inventory of PCs at outlets that needed to be off-loaded before new products were introduced during the summer. Thoman then dropped prices on IBM's inventory, setting off a price war with Compaq. He also launched a large advertising campaign for the new Aptiva PC and Butterfly laptops to attract back-to-school and Christmas customers. This campaign was more successful than IBM had anticipated and created a significant pent-up demand for both PCs.

In June 1994, R & D problems emerged with both of the new computers, delaying their launch beyond the back-to-school season. When Thoman attempted to increase production to meet the accumulating demand, manufacturing and supplier problems developed and angry customers turned to other PC makers. IBM's PC market shares dropped from 18 in 1993 to 5 percent in 1994. IBM watched as Compaq, Apple, and Packard Bell passed them in market shares. IBM's PC unit lost $1 billion in 1994. This in turn led to the departure of Thoman's top two assistants, the general manager and head of manufacturing for the PC unit (Ziegler 1995, B1).

At the same time, in June of 1994 IBM's PC unit announced the development of a new generation of PCs to be built on IBM's new power chip, which was 25 percent faster than PCs based on Intel's new Pentium chip, and a new OS/2 Warp operating system which was to challenge Microsoft's Windows. However, IBM was a year late in reaching production with its new chip and this allowed Intel to bring out an advanced Pentium chip, which cut IBM's speed and advantage by 10 percent. In addition OS/2 Warp was a year behind schedule and IBM had to use Microsoft Windows as an operating system (Kim 1995, 68).

By 1995 Thoman had made several moves designed to improve the PC unit's performance. *First*, he transferred the PC servers function to another unit, allowing the PC unit to focus its concerns on PCs alone. *Second*, he divided the remaining PC unit into two parts, one focusing on the business and the other on the consumer markets. *Third*, he hired two new CEOs from outside IBM to head each function. Samuel Palmisano would head the business PC function and James Firestone would head the consumer PC function. *Fourth*, teams were set up to reengineer the PC unit's R & D, manufacturing supply, and marketing functions. *Fifth*, Thoman cut IBM's PC manufacturing lines from nine to five and consolidated their operations, eliminating 2,000 jobs, which was 20 percent of the unit's workforce (Kim 1995, B6). Thoman then announced to stockholders that the solution to the unit's problems were two to three years away. Making all these changes at once left the PC unit in disarray (Hill 1995, R4). IBM's new products for the PC market—the OS/2Warp operating system, the Activa, and the Butterfly computers—would be outdated in two years. Product life cycles in the PC market were 8 to 12 months. The R & D costs involved in developing and marketing new products would make the PC unit unprofitable for several years (Zuckerman, 1995, D4).

By the end of 1996, IBM's PC business function under Palmisano appeared to have reached a watershed in solving its problems. The PC unit's sales grew to $12.5 billion and profits from the business function were back, but the consumer market still lost big money. IBM's market share rose from 5 percent to 8.9 percent, placing IBM number 2 to Compaq world wide. Gerstner was so pleased by Palmisano's performance he elevated him to vice president and expanded his duties. While the business PC function was doing well, the consumer function was still experiencing difficulties in estimating customer demand, driving the PC unit's overall profits $39 million in the red. This loss was due to aggressive price cutting by IBM's competitors, which IBM matched dollar for dollar (Ziegler 1997, B1).

1997 was a difficult year for IBM's PC unit. *First*, the PC market was shifting dramatically towards the Internet. In an attempt to be responsive to this shift, IBM developed a prototype network PC. This network PC was a stripped-down version of IBM's Aptiva PC and had a $1,200 price tag without a monitor. IBM's competitors brought out new network PCs with monitors for $900, $600, and $500. In September of 1997, IBM withdrew from the production and marketing of its network PC, citing lack of customer demand as the reason for halting production (Narisetti 1997, A3).

Second, the PC unit employed its newly restructured manufacturing, supply, and marketing functions to expand its inventory of Aptiva and Butterfly computers in salesrooms for back-to-school and Christmas sales. In late 1996 and early 1997, Dell, with its direct marketing model, made a dramatic push for increased market share by lowering PC prices. In an attempt to halt declining market shares, IBM matched its competitors' prices at a considerable loss per sale.

Third, in addition, 40 percent of consumer sales from outlets during this year were for network PCs costing under $1,000, of which IBM had none. IBM's sales outlets were left with a 120-day inventory of IBM PCs (Narisetti 1997, B1). The PC unit responded to this inventory problem by cutting prices on all PCs below those of its competitors and offering outlets sales incentives in an attempt to reduce inventory and maintain market share. These price cuts created a significant loss on each sale in the consumer market and affected prices on Aptiva and Butterfly PCs in the business market.

Fourth, the PC unit once again set up teams to a cut IBM costs 5 to 15 percent. In addition it cut the number of PC wholesalers from over 100 to 11. Next IBM asked these wholesalers to help assemble computers at no cost (Narisetti 1997, B8). By the end of 1997, IBM's consumer PC business market share had dropped dramatically from 14.4 percent in 1996 to 4.4 percent. In addition, dealer inventories still remained high. The PC unit's profits for the year ran $161 million in the red (Burrows and Sager 1999, 150).

Thus between 1994 and 1997, IBM's PC unit experienced significant R & D, manufacturing, supply, and marketing problems. The PC unit had set up teams on several occasions to restructure, cut headcount, and cut costs and yet were still having major performance problems. The PC unit ran $1 billion, $39 million, and $161 million in the red for 1995, 1996, and 1997. These performance issues led several stock analysts to suggest that IBM consider dropping or outsourcing to Dell their PC unit functions in order to improve their overall competitive position (Narisetti 1997, B1).

IBM's PC Unit's Benchmarking of Dell Computer Corporation's Performance in 1998

Pricing pressures will be similar (in the PC market) and we will be very responsive. We are going through a difficult period, but we feel much better about our competitiveness and our business processes.

L. Ricciardi, IBM CFO, (Hansell, 1998:D2)

1998 involved three constructive moves for IBM's PC unit. *First*, the PC unit had just completed several years of teamwork aimed at improving its supplier, manufacturing, and distribution functions. These teams had succeeded in simplifying and reducing the unit's cost structure (see table 6.1).

In 1998, IBM's PC unit undertook several steps aimed at a turnaround. First, in 1995 IBM had hired a Dell supply expert to help decrease its inventory of parts. By 1998 he had succeeded in cutting IBM's parts inventory from 5 days to 24 hours for 60 percent of PC parts. As a result, IBM's inventory turns have gone from 3 per year in 1994 to 15 per year in 1997 (Narisetti 1998, B1). In 1998 about 31 percent of IBM's PCs were assembled by 11 business partners. IBM now sells several computers on the Internet. However, it could not configure them to the customer's specifications. Thus IBM's PC unit had clearly improved dramatically over its own 1994 performance levels. However, it did not improve as much as some of its competitors.

Table 6.1
Making More Out of Less: Changes in Products,
Manufacturing Processes, and Workforce at IBM

	1997	1994
Models assembled at IBM plants	150	3,400
Available options	350	750
Types of major components	200	400
Variety of parts in inventory	15,000	56,000
Parts replenished daily by suppliers	62%	5%
Percent of U.S. PCs assembled by distributors	31%	0%
PC unit employees worldwise	9,241	10,000

Source: R. Narisetti, "How IBM turned around its ailing PC division," *Wall Street Journal,* March 12, 1998, B1.

In 1998 IBM's sales improved 18 percent over 1997, with the PC unit running $992 million in the red due to a price war with its competitors (Burrows and Sager 1999, 150).

Second, in July 1998, IBM replaced James Firestone, the head of the PC consumer function, and folded servers and mobile functions back into the PC unit (Hansell 1998, D2).

Third, the PC unit benchmarked the world-class performance of the Dell Computer Corporation (see table 6.2). At the time of this benchmarking effort IBM's PC unit did not have a VAE of $74,500+ per employee nor an ROA of 7 percent.

It is obvious from the data in Table 6.2 that Dell has a substantial advantage over IBM in market share, Internet sales, time to convert sales to cash, average retailer costs and incentives, computer delivery time, parts inventory, network installation time, and continuous-improvement savings. IBM has a significantly larger service force. In 1998 this allowed Dell's sales to increase 48 percent compared to IBM's 16 percent, its profit margins to reach more than 22 percent or $2 billion while IBM lost $1 billion (a loss similar to 1994), and its market shares to reach 11.9 percent while IBM's held at 7.5 percent. Once again market analysts call for IBM to drop its PC function or outsource it to Dell in order to increase profitability (Sager 1998, 52).

In spite of major downsizings, restructurings, and management changes in 1994, 1995, 1996, 1997, and 1998, by July of 1999, IBM's PC unit was well on its way to another billion-dollar loss. In July of 1999, Robert Moffet Jr. took over as head of the PC unit. He immediately undertook several important changes. First, he jetti-

Table 6.2
Comparison of Dell and IBM Business Practices, 1998

	Dell	IBM
PC market share	11.8%	7.5%
Internet sales	90%	20%
Time to convert sale to cash	1 day	25 days
Average retailer cost	0	20%
Average sales incentives	0	$1000
Delivery time for internet sales	3.1 days	15 days
Parts inventory	15 minutes	5 days
Computer inventory	3 days	35 days
Average network installation time	14 days	60 days
Continuous-improvement savings	20%	15%
Service corporation size	10,000	40,000

soned the flagging business of selling PC's in retail stores and focused on the more profitable corporate sales. Second, he expanded the sale of PCs over the Internet. This allowed the PC unit to obtain one quarter of its revenues from the Internet by 2000 (Buckeley 2000, B1). Third, the new Think Pad laptop computer took the global lead from Toshiba in sales. Fourth, he expanded the use of mini warehouses near IBM assembly plants so suppliers could deliver parts 3 hours before their use, saving $100 million per year in inventory costs. Fifth, he redesigned products to use standardized parts, saving $300 million per year. Seventh, he cut 10 percent of the workforce.

The result of these changes was that in 1999, the PC unit lost $400 million. However, by the final two quarters of 2000, the PC unit showed a $99 million profit. IBM ranked fourth in the world PC market in 2000 with a 6.8 percent market share, down from 9.8 percent in 1999, and ranked fifth in the U.S. with a 5.4 percent market share, down from 7.3 percent a year earlier (Buckeley 2001, B1). After seven years of downsizing, restructuring, and management changes, IBM's PC unit still does not meet Ernst and Young's standard of a VAE of $74,000 per employee and an ROA of 7 percent, nor has the PC unit been able to implement the best practices of the Dell Computer Corporation from its 1998 benchmarking study.

Between 1994 and 2000, IBM's PC unit lost over $3.2 billion, cut over 6,000 jobs, and realigned its management team several times. This data led Andrew Neff, an analyst with Bear Sterns, to suggest that, having finally made a profit in the last two quarters of 2000,

"They can declare victory and go home" and should sell the PC unit to a competitor and move on (Buckeley 2001, B1). The cost of improving the PC unit's performance when weighed against the profit potential of the unit appears to be hardly worth the effort.

Conclusions Regarding Ernst and Young's Claim in the IBM PC Unit Case

The PC era is over.

Louis Gerstner, CEO (IBM 1998 Annual Report)

This is a conclusion Gerstner reached after watching IBM's PC unit lose $1 billion, $39 million, $161 million, and $992 million in the years 1994–1998. However IBM's PC unit is still in place, still attempting to improve its performance, and still developing new products. Several conclusions can be drawn from our inquiry.

First, it is difficult to draw hard and fast conclusions regarding IBM's PC unit's success in benchmarking and implementing changes in its own unit four years after it completed its benchmarking effort. However, several trends appear clear. IBM had made significant progress over its own 1994 performance standards in all the areas outlined above. It is equally clear that in 1998 Dell outperformed IBM in 2000 in all but one benchmarking area. It is also clear that Dell is increasing its continuous-improvement savings at 20 percent per year over its 1998 world-class performance levels. In addition, IBM's PC unit earnings between 1998 and 2000 were $2 billion in the red while Dell is experiencing larger profit margins.

Second, while this is only one case, it appears that Ernst and Young's claim that to successfully benchmark world-class performance requires a higher level of VAE and ROA than IBM's PC unit had is supported. Organizational learning requires a level of organizational competence not yet present in IBM's PC unit (Burrows and Sager 1999, 150).

Third, after years of downsizing, restructuring, and management changes, many competent IBM workers and managers have left for other organizations. This further depletes the learning capability of those who remain.

Fourth, the cost of bringing an underperforming unit up to world-class best practices standards may in the long run not be worth the effort required.

Fifth, several issues that require further inquiry are raised by this case study. When the rate of continuous-improvement savings by a world-class performer is greater than that of the firm benchmarking them, can they ever be expected to catch up? When a firm has a low VAE or ROA, can repeated changes in leadership be expected to substantially increase worker performance without substantial improvement in workers' training and learning capabilities? Is high learning capability in some parts of a unit's value chain always offset by low learning capabilities in another part of the value chain?

Finally, in January of 2002, IBM, the company that put the PC on the map, announced it would no longer manufacture desktop PCs in most of the world. The decision marks the latest step in IBM's retreat from the PC business. Unable to compete against low-cost leader Dell, IBM's PC group has lost money and market shares for years (Buckeley 2002, B1). In January 2002, IBM reported a $136 million loss for its latest quarter and its PC market shares dropped to 54 percent, placing it behind Dell, Compaq, and Hewlett-Packard. This drop occurred in spite of IBM's PC unit cutting costs 30 percent (Buckeley 2002, B1).

Our task in this inquiry has been clear: to investigate the effects of an organization's or unit of an organization's learning capabilities as a limiting factor in benchmarking and implementing world-class performance. Our findings have been clear in the case of IBM's PC unit: the learning capabilities of employees have been a limiting factor in its benchmarking and implementation of Dell's world-class performance. Several important and interesting issues have emerged. The rate of continuous-improvement savings by one's competitors and a world-class benchmark may prevent catching up. Leadership change may not work unless a poorly performing firm can upgrade the learning capabilities of its workers. Low learning capabilities in one part of a firm's value chain may offset excellent learning in all other parts of a value chain.

References

Buckeley, W. (2001). IBM turns around its PC unit, though skeptics still call it a drag. *Wall Street Journal*, February 15, B1.

———. (2002). As PC industry slumps, IBM hands off manufacturing of desktops. *Wall Street Journal*, January 7, B4.

Burrows, P., and Sager, I. (1999). PC makers think beyond the box. *Business Week*, April 19, 148–150.

Camp, R. (1992). Learning from the best leads to superior performance. *Journal of Business Strategy* (July): 3–5.

Hansell, S. (1998). I.B.M. shifts chief of PCs for consumer. *New York Times*, July 23.

Hays, L. (1995). IBM is "gathering momentum," Gerstner says at annual meeting. *Wall Street Journal*, April 26, B6.

Hill, G. C. (1995). Packard Bell led the U.S. PC market in first quarter: IBM bouncing back. *Wall Street Journal*, May 1, B4.

IBM (1998). *Annual Report.*

Kim, J. (1995). IBM tries to revitalize its PC business. *USA Today*, June 19, 6B.

Lohr, S. (2002). IBM says earnings to fall short of estimates. *New York Times*, April 9, C4.

Narisetti, R. (1997). IBM retreats from selling simple Net PCs. *Wall Street Journal*, September 8, A3, A8.

———. (1997). IBM to revamp struggling home-PC business. *Wall Street Journal*, October 14, B1, B12.

———. (1998). How IBM turned around its ailing PC division. *Wall Street Journal*, March 12, B1, B6.

———. (1998). IBM plan aims to cut dealers' PC costs, boost services to combat Dell, Compaq. *Wall Street Journal*, September 15, B8.

Port, O., Cary, U., Kelley, K., and Forrest, F. (1993). Quality. *Business Week*, November 30, 66–74.

Sager, I. (1998). Big Blue should get a little smaller. *Business Week*, September 14, 52–53.

———. (1999). Inside IBM: Internet business machines. *Business Week*, December 13, EB23.

Sager, I., McWilliams, G., and Reinhardt, A. (1998). IBM: Back to double-digit growth? *Business Week*, June 1, 116–120.

Sherman, S. (1994). Is he too cautious to save IBM? *Fortune*, October 3, 78–90.

Waga, P. (1997). IBM reboots home PC unit. *USA Today*, October 15, B2.

Ziegler, B. (1995). IBM tries, and fails, to fix PC business. *Wall Street Journal*, February 22, B1, B6.

————. (1997). Gerstner's IBM revival: Impressive, incomplete. *Wall Street Journal*, March 25, B1, B4.

————. (1997). IBM shuffles jobs, elevating PC executive. *Wall Street Journal*, July 23, A3, A6.

Zuckerman, L. (1995). IBM surpasses forecasts but it drops by 25 cents a share. *New York Times*, July 19, D4.

7

Time as a Limiting Factor:
A Case Study of the Danville Bumper Works

Benchmarking's benefits as a strategic planning method are that it identifies the key to success for each area studied, provides specific quantitative targets to shoot for, creates an awareness of state-of-the art approaches, and helps companies cultivate a culture where change, adaptation, and continuous improvement are actively sought out.

(Altany, 1990:14)

It also requires patience, perseverance, and, more often than not, time to work through, in interactive communication, the process of adapting what has been learned to one's own organization in order to meet the firm's own targets and goals as well as those with whom the firm may have an alliance. When there are two firms involved, the question of time becomes even more crucial.

Interactively Defining the Operation

In 1978 Mr. Shahid Khan, a naturalized U.S. citizen from Pakistan and a mechanical engineer with a degree from the University of Illinois, quit his job with Flex-a-Gate, confident his invention of a low-cost truck bumper design was the best. He borrowed $50,000 from the Small Business Administration and took $13,000 of his own savings to establish the 100-employee Bumper Works in Danville, Illinois. In two years, by 1980, Mr. Kahn had bought out his old employer.

For five years, between 1980 and 1985, Mr. Khan approached the Toyota Motor Corporation in an attempt to become a supplier of bumpers for their trucks. He landed his first contract with Toyota in 1985. In 1987 Toyota called together a group of 100 potential suppliers and released its design, quality, quantity, and price range specifications for the product and told Mr. Khan and two other bumper makers to design new bumpers much more durable than the Big Three specifications required. Mr. Khan noted with elation, "We were the only ones who could demonstrate we could do that." And in 1988, Mr. Khan's firm became the sole supplier of bumpers to U.S. Toyota facilities at which rear bumpers and other accessories were attached to trucks made in Japan.

Interactively Restructuring the Original Agreement

But the honeymoon was short lived. Toyota wanted more in the way of price reductions, although the costs for materials and labor had risen. They wanted increased quality, reduction in time of delivery, and a reduction in price from the supplier each year. In 1989, in order to demonstrate what they wanted, Toyota Motors flew Mr. Khan and one of his aides to Japan to see the production system firsthand and when there were no results from this meeting, in 1989 sent a manufacturing expert from Toyota headquarters to help. It was clear that nothing could be done until Bumper Works switched its factory from a mass production to a batch production line and that a massive stamping machine which took 90 minutes to change each cutting die would have to be modified so as to make such changes in 20 minutes.

The workers at both Bumper Works and Toyota set up teams to make a process map of current production procedures. They studied, simplified, and restructured the process so as to allow for batch production. The large stamping machine was studied for modifications that would speed up die changes. The Bumper Works could not afford a major overhaul so the workers improvised by welding homemade metal tabs to their nine-ton dies that made alignment easier. All this was done with considerable help from Toyota, which had solved these same problems, but in a different way, back in Japan.

Finally the Bumper Works' remodeled assembly line was ready to begin production and be refined to meet the quality and time specifications of Toyota. For six months employees with stop watches and cost sheets observed the restructured process and benchmarked its operations against the world-class standards of the Toyota plant in Japan. They videotaped the process, studied it, and sent the videotapes to Japan for review. In July 1990 Toyota sent a team to help retrain the workers. It was "boot camp" time. Equipment was moved, 16-hour days were the norm, jobs had to be relearned. Two of the six supervisors at Bumper Works quit in frustration.

Interactively Fine Tuning the Production Line

Toyota's consultants returned in December of 1990 to fine tune the process again in order to meet Toyota's contract requirements. This new production line increased productivity over 60 percent above the previous year, decreased defects 80 percent, cut delivery time by 850 percent, and cut waste materials cost by 50 percent. A manual and videotape of the manufacturing process were prepared for training, the first of their kind at Bumper Works, and continuous-improvement teams were formed in order to meet Toyota's contract requirements of increased quality and decreased costs. The employees at Bumper Works scheduled their own work rather than wait for a supervisor to give directions. The changes sound simple, but Khan was still consulting Toyota as problems arose. "They call it open kimono discussion," said Mr. Khan, "but I call it no kimono." The communication process was ongoing, open, and noncombative.

The representatives of each unit involved in the value chain linking Bumper Works and Toyota communicated their interests, concerns, and contributions to the coalignment process. Each firm's management, therefore, was able to forge a linking process that was satisfactory and optimizing in the value-added activities of each organization, creating a sustainable competitive advantage. Mr. Khan profited from this experience. He added 200 workers to his new factory in Indiana, which would continue to supply Toyota but would add Isuzu Motors, with ambitions to service the Big Three.

Interactively Agreeing that the Benchmark Had Been Implemented

In five years—from the time of Mr. Khan's first contract with Toyota to the time when Toyota declared their bumpers as meeting their specifications of quality, price, and delivery time—Mr. Khan went from his original $64,000 investment to $40 million. But it took continual benchmarking, a continual willingness to change, continual open communication, and a conception of long-term pay-off for this alliance to succeed.

> More and more of the world's goods require not the standardized and modest quality associated with mass production but continuous innovations and thus design and production changes and higher quality. Change and quality in turn requires different organizational structures and small practices: decentralized structures, small-firm networks, or subcontractors that are not dependent and exploited, and work practices in which conception and execution come together once more.
>
> (Perrow 1992, 163)

References

Altany, D. (1990). Copy cats. *Industry Week,* November 5, 11–18.

Perrow, C. (1992). Review of the M. Best "The new competition: Institutions of industrial restructuring." *Administrative Science Quarterly,* (March): 162–166.

White, J. (1991). Japanese auto maker helps U.S. suppliers become more efficient. *Wall Street Journal,* September 9.

8

Culture as a Limiting Factor:
A Case Study of ABB

Organizational culture is the pattern of basic assumptions that a given group has invested, discovered, or developed in learning to cope with its problems of external adaptation and internal integration, and that have worked well enough to be considered valid and therefore, to be taught to new members as the correct way to perceive, think, and feel in relation to those problems.

(Shein, 1984:3)

At the core of an organization's integration, coordination, and control processes are its prescriptive values, rules, reward and punishment systems—its corporate culture. A culture is a complex of values which contains a vision of that culture's ideal of excellence (Weaver 1964). A culture in this sense is an orientation system from which the most powerful and humble members can borrow to give dignity, direction, and a sense of belonging to their lives. From within a culture's vision—this ideal of its own excellence—comes the power of the culture to inspire and to motivate significant effort. A culture is by nature restrictive. It provides a preferred viewpoint on the world and asks its members to seek out and establish their personal identity within that vision, or experience the threat of the primary reference group's denying the validity of their existence.

A corporate culture serves at least three functions: legitimation, motivation, and integration. *First*, a culture provides its members with a firm's legitimate patterns of interpretation and behavior for dealing with culturally relevant problems. *Second*, a culture provides its members with a hierarchy of values, a motivational structure which links the identity of individuals to culturally relevant roles and values. *Third*, a culture provides its members with a symbolically integrated framework that regulates social interaction and goal attainment through the creation of cultural messages (Gutknecht 1982).

It will be the purpose of this chapter to indicate how and why an organization's corporate culture can limit the effectiveness of its benchmarking process. We will develop this analysis in four stages: (1) We will examine the ABB's (ABB) corporate culture; (2) we will explore ABB's 1993 benchmarking study of the General Electric Corporation; (3) we will explore ABB's initial and later response to that benchmarking process; and (4) we will draw some conclusions regarding the limitations a firm's corporate culture can place on its benchmarking processes. Let us address each of these issues in turn.

ABB Corporate Culture

What gives me a sense of reward is to create something, to make a kind of lasting impression. I don't work for money or prestige and all that. People want to build something that is worthwhile. That is what it boils down to.

Percy Barnevik, CEO, ABB, (Vries, 1994:32)

In 1987, the Swedish electric firm, Asea, with a strong presence in the Scandinavian market, merged with its Swiss counterpart, Brown and Boveri, an electric engineering firm with a strong presence in the Swiss and German markets, to create Asea Brown Boveri, now called ABB. This merger was crafted and then led by one man, Percy Barnevik. In 1987, times were changing in important ways in Europe. The European Economic Community was coming into being, aimed at uniting the central countries of Europe into a community capable of competing with the United States and Asia in a very competitive global economy. The Soviet Union's hold on Eastern Europe and its own union of states were falling apart and several of those newly freed nations were looking towards Europe for stronger ties and to help lead them out of communism and socialism into representative democracies and capitalism in order to obtain the economic benefits of a global economy. Barnevik choose this moment in time to propose the creation of a new, uniquely European multinational whose intent was to develop pride in Europe's unique contribution to the global economy and ABB's unique contribution to European pride (Cushman and King 1994, 94–117).

The vision Barnevik presented of this new company was of a firm in which ABB employees could feel pride and see something of value, a firm that went beyond the numbers provided by sales, profits, and stockholder value figures. ABB was to be a firm committed to (1) respect for cultural diversity, which at the same time integrated this cultural diversity into a creative and effective organization; (2) pioneering the investment in training of and productively integrating the nations and people of the former socialist block and Soviet Union into the new European community and capitalist economic system; and (3) cleaning up the environment by developing environmentally sound equipment and manufacturing processes. In so doing ABB employees could join with Barnevik in building something of value, changing the world in a positive way, and creating a uniquely European firm (kets de Vries 1994, 30).

Initially ABB was structured into eight business segments: electrical power distribution, electrical power transmission, electrical transportation, environmental control, financial services, industrial engineering, and a group of smaller support firms. Most of ABB's sales in power equipment, rail equipment, pollution control, and industrial engineering were made directly to governments and public utilities. This new European multinational company would compete with the German industrial giant Siemens, Britain's GEC, and over forty smaller national firms. Creating a multinational electrical engineering firm in the European market confronted ABB with several significant challenges to which Barnevik had to respond in a constructive way if ABB was to build "something of value" (Taylor 1991, 105).

First, a strong national preference existed for electrical products and services which was such an ingrained habit in Europe that local producers had a definite advantage. In addition, national regulation of and standards for these products and services further reinforced this ingrained habit of purchasing them from local producers (Taylor 1991, 105).

Second, the large R & D costs involved in developing state-of-the-art nuclear, gas, steam, and electrical generators; high speed electrical trains; and effective environmental control processes was such that large multinational firms like the General Electric and Westinghouse companies from America and the Hitachi and Mitsubishi companies from Japan were developing high-quality, low-priced products which were making inroads into the European market (Taylor 1991, 105).

Third, in order to compete effectively in such an environment, a new multinational firm had to be technically skilled, organizationally efficient, and adaptive to changing customer needs to update old and expensive equipment, to finance new state of the art equipment, and to provide quick and response service in both of these areas (Taylor 1991, 105).

In an attempt to operationalize this vision and respond to these three competitive pressures in the marketplace, Barnevik undertook three organizational strategies. *First*, Barnevik sought to acquire, merge, and form joint ventures with nationally recognized local firms with a reputation for quality and service in each of ABB's major regional markets in order to be responsive to the ingrained habit of preferring local firms who were adapted to local regulations (Kennedy 1992, 25). *Second,* Barnevik immediately restructured these acquisitions, mergers, and joint ventures to make the firms lean, mean, and agile, and to update their technical and management skills, and to transfer state-of-the-art technology. Here Barnevik argues that 30 percent of a firm's employees can be spun off into new independent service firms, 30 percent absorbed into the core operating unit, and 30 percent let go while 10 percent remain to manage the firm. The 40 percent of employees who remain then benchmark one of ABB's centers of excellence firms which mentor the new firm and the change process. *Third,* these new ABB firms are put online in ABB's unique matrix management system. ABB's management system is a top down administrative and control system where each local firm is responsive to two managers, a business area manager, and a regional or country manager (see figure 8.1).

Figure 8.1
ABB's Management Communication System

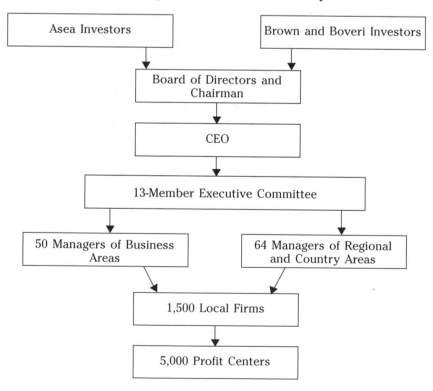

At the top are the investors, board of directors, CEO Barnevik, and an executive committee who are responsible for global strategy, R & D, and resourcing. At the bottom are the business area managers and regional and country managers and profit centers responsible for local performance. ABB's three-stage strategy of acquisition, downsizing, and top-down matrix management was designed by Barnevik to overcome the several contradictions presented by ABB's competitive marketplace. These contradictions were to become global and local, big and small, centralized and decentralized at the same time while achieving ABB's vision of respecting and integrating cultural diversity, investing in integrating Eastern Europe and the former Soviet Union into the European Community and capitalism, and developing environmentally friendly equipment and services. ABB's seven-year performance record is presented in table 8.1 below.

Under the leadership of Barnevik ABB quickly became one of the most respected multinationals in Europe. In 1995 the company was selected to the Best of the Best in Europe for its enlightened vision, management of technology, and innovative management system in a poll conducted by the Arthur Little Consulting firm. It was selected Europe's Most Respected firm in a poll conducted by the *Financial Times*. ABB was considered "a modern industrial model for the future" by the McKinsey's Consulting firm. It was voted by students enrolled in European MBA programs as their most preferred firm for which to work. In addition Barnevik was named manager of the year and leader of the year in Europe, and was considered one of the most effective leaders in the world (Gibson 1995, 19).

In 1994 Percy Barnevik summarized his and ABB's success when he stated,

> To continue the momentum of change, it is important that our people feel pride in something beyond the numbers. For example, we have pioneered investments in Eastern Europe, spearheading East-West integration. I don't want to claim that we

Table 8.1
ABB's Seven-Year Performance Record: 1992–1999
in millions of dollars

	2001	2000	1999	1998	1997	1996	1995
Sales	23,726	22,967	24,682	23,734	31,265	33,767	32,751
Profits	–691	1,433	1,615	1,305	572	1,233	1,315

Source: *ABB Financial Facts*, 2002

knew more than anyone else, but I was absolutely convinced that Eastern Europe would open up. Consequently, because we were the first, we had the pick of the best Polish companies. Many of our people are proud of participating in that process. The same can be said about our work in the environmental field. I would like to create and develop an image of us helping to improve the world environment. For example, transferring sustainable technology to China or India, where they have a tremendous need to clean up their coal-fired plants.

Our employees can look at work like that and see that we contribute something beyond mere shareholder value. This is particularly relevant for attracting young people to the company. By and large, they are not happy just to work for a big company with high profits; they also like to see a purpose that goes beyond numbers. It is important that a company be perceived as changing the world in a positive way. (in Kets de Vries 1994, 30)

ABB's Benchmarking of the General Electric Company

It's not a matter of getting it right the first time, it's a matter of continuously changing to keep it right.

(Berling, 1993:16)

Success is a two-edged sword. It invites, and ABB and CEO Percy Barnevik received, accolades and recognition throughout Europe in particular and the world in general. Success also invites comparisons with the best of the best and criticism for less than world-class performance when such comparisons are made. ABB and its CEO Percy Barnevik, while receiving accolades and respect from colleagues in Europe, were beginning to be compared with the General Electric Company and its CEO Jack Welch in the United States, and that comparison focused attention on GE's superior innovations, performance, and management skills (see chapter 3 of this book). So in 1993, ABB and Percy Barnevik commissioned a benchmarking study of GE and Jack Welch.

The objectives of that benchmarking study were (1) to give a brief overview of selected large ABB competitors in the electrotechnical field; (2) to show why GE is the most important company for ABB to understand and maybe learn from; (3) to describe some aspects of the transformation GE has been going through over the past several years; and (4) to support the customer-focus program with a benchmarking annotation towards it (Harnischfeger, Von Der Wense, and Hagan 1993).

Why was GE selected as the benchmark? Because GE consistently earned more profits than ABB, Hitachi, Siemens, Mitsubishi, Toshiba, and GEC Alstom, its six largest competitors in the electrotechnical market, combined. In 1992, GE earned $7.7 billion in profits. These other six firms combined earned $6.8 billion in profits. GE's profit margins were between 15 and 20 percent while the next best competitor earned 8 percent. During the last eight years, GE had outgrown its competitors in size while being the only firm to reduce its workforce. GE's market capitalization was three times larger than that of its next best competitor, Hitachi, and eight times larger than ABB's. GE's market value per employee was ten times larger than ABB's.

The results of this benchmarking study were perplexing for ABB. What they found was a direct clash between GE and ABB in regard to vision, management systems, and culture. GE had a vision of being a lean, mean, rapid-response organization based on worker, supplier, and customer input which created high profits and stockholder value. GE was not very diverse culturally, it had little or no interest in the Eastern Block and former Soviet Union, and it frequently polluted the environments in which it operated. GE had a bottom-up management system which allowed open competition between GE businesses and encouraged entrepreneurial, innovative, and risk-taking activities. ABB had a top-down management system which prevented open competition between units by allocating specific markets to firms and which was conservative in encouraging entrepreneurial risk-taking activities. GE was a rapid-response, customer-focused firm. ABB proceeded surely but slowly and was a technology-driven, politically controlled, functionally organized firm in responding to customer needs.

Faced with these findings, ABB's benchmarking study concluded that GE's success was not due to the selection of GE businesses, to its acquisition strategy, to the extensive use of business synergies, to aggressive efforts at globalization, or to the aggressive use of foreign labor. According to Harnishberger, Von Der Wense, and Hagan (1993), GE only created a mix of

- a vision that is credibly communicated and lived,

- very tough objectives set from the top,

- rapid decision making with limited analysis,

- rapid implementation by empowered employees,

- continuous push for improvement and change,

- short feedback and learning cycles, and

- delegation and ownership where it belonged.

Three things should be noted regarding the conclusions ABB drew from this benchmarking study.

First, the conclusions are all top-down conclusions about what a CEO should do.

Second, ABB failed to grasp how GE's workout, rapid-response communication systems, and culture ensured bottom-up entrepreneurial, innovative, and risk-taking activities by suppliers, workers, and customers.

Third, ABB completely disregarded the various implementing structures GE put in place to ensure effectiveness in implementing its lived vision, tough objectives, rapid decision making, rapid implementation, continuous push for change, and short feedback and ownership cycles.

In short, the benchmarking study failed to identify the critical success factor for GE's performance because of ABB's top-down culture, and this in spite of ABB's high learning capability, which met Ernst and Young's highest standards, and when ABB had a potentially long time line.

What did all this mean to ABB? It meant that ABB could achieve a lot more regarding profits, new business opportunities, and culture.

It also meant that ABB had to focus on processes and people instead of functions and politics by serving customers, managing and pushing business, fostering change, and globalizing the company (Harnishfeger, Von Der Wense, and Hagan 1993).

The benchmarking report was circulated to a very limited number of top management officials; no follow-up or implementing procedures were undertaken to utilize the benchmarking process. To do so would have called into question ABB's vision, management system, and corporate culture as well as Barnevik's and ABB's public recognition of ABB's unique European perspective, and ABB would not seriously consider such an outcome.

Between 1994 and 1997, ABB rationalized its global holdings, making significant acquisitions in Eastern Europe and the former Soviet Union. ABB moved 40,000 jobs from the United States and Western Europe into Eastern Europe, and began a major move into Asia. All of this was designed to fulfill its vision of creating a culturally diverse set of managers and employees, integrating ABB operations in Eastern Europe and the Soviet Union into its Western European operations, and undertaking several significant environmental control projects. On January 1, 1999, Barnevik stepped down as CEO of ABB, proclaiming that his vision had been fulfilled and ABB was doing well. He retained his position as chairman of the board of directors and took another CEO job elsewhere. He was succeeded as CEO by his longtime friend and assistant, Goran Lindahl.

Between 1997 and 1999, Lindahl, taking a leaf out of GE's book, immediately set about the task of restructuring ABB's sluggish management system, antiquated capital structure, and accounting system and to refocus ABB product lines in high-margin, high-growth businesses. He promised to move ABB from $33 billion to $50 billion in sales and from 4.2 to 7 percent profit margins by 2001 (Hall and Marshall 1998, 185).

In his major restructuring between 1997 and 2000, Lindahl (Morris 1999, 61) acquired Elsaq Bailey, an Italian process automation firm, for $2.1 billion, creating an $8.5 billion a year automation division for ABB. He sold ABB's 50 percent stake in its railway business to Daimler-Chrysler for $472 million, withdrawing from a low-margin business. He spun off ABB's low-margin power generation division into a joint venture with Alstom, a French company, receiving $1.5 billion and a 50 percent interest in the new ABB/Alstom, an $8 billion a year firm. He then sold ABB's 50 percent interest to Alston for $1.2 billion, withdrawing from a second low-margin business (Woodruff 2000, A24). He closed 12 factories in Europe and cut another 13,000 employees to save $30 million. He cut 100 regional managers and reordered ABB's management structure from a matrix to 7 operating businesses in new high-margin areas: (1) automation, (2) oil, gas, and petrochemicals, (3) products and contracts, (4) power transmission, (5) power distribution, (6) financial services, and (7) competitive activities. He raised ABB's targets on profit margins from 1.8 percent to 7 percent by 2000. He restructured ABB's stock shares from 4 types to 1, leading to a 100 percent rise in share price. He focused ABB's R & D efforts in the automation and the oil, gas, and petrochemical areas. He then developed a new division of financial services to handle mortgages. In 1999, profits bounced back with a 31 percent increase and ABB's stock price doubled, closing at $116 per share (Fleming 1999, A8).

Finally, in 1999 Goran Lindahl agreed to head a second benchmarking study of GE to be undertaken by the Performance Group, an Anglo-Norwegian consultancy group (Burt 1999, A10).

The benchmarking study was motivated by GE's performance between 1994 and 1999. GE sales rose from $63 billion to $111 billion, and profits rose from $4.8 to $10.7 billion. GE's European sales rose from $10 billion to $40 billion with profit margins approaching 30 percent. In that same time frame, ABB's global sales went from $28 billion to $22 billion, with profit margins approaching 7 percent (Woodruff 2000, 12). The benchmarking study drew the following conclusions (Burt 1999, 6):

- The long term organic growth enjoyed by GE depends on continual breakthroughs in every area from product development to corporate culture, from sales and marketing to labor relations.

- The major cultural change at GE was getting people to accept that it's OK to step out of their comfort zone, which is the way they have always done things, and to be willing to take a risk on trying something new.

- Error management coupled with an appetite for risk and innovation were essential factors for a breakthrough-conducive environment.

Three things should again be noted regarding the conclusions drawn from this benchmarking study:

First, conclusions again are all top-down conclusions regarding what a CEO should do.

Second, again the benchmarking study failed to identify the sources of breakthroughs as workers, suppliers, customers, and best practice.

Third, the study completely disregarded the various implementing structures which GE put in place to generate breakthroughs and rapid cultural change (see chapter 3 on GE).

What ABB will do as a result of these conclusions has only recently become clear. However, ABB's shift away from low-growth, low-margin businesses towards high-growth, high-margin businesses was a beginning and a major cultural change, but it may not be directly attributable to ABB's benchmarking of GE. In a surprise move to investors, on October 26, 2000, Lindahl, then 55, announced his intention to resign as CEO effective January 1, 2001, with two years remaining on his contract. He cited as his reason for leaving the need for a younger leader who understood the role information technology needed to play in ABB's development (Hall and Marsh, 2000, B2). The results of Lindahl's four-year tenure as ABB's CEO were mixed. Between 1996 and 2000, ABB's sales declined from $33.7 billion to $22.9 billion, while profits rose from $1.2 billiion to $1.3 billion, with stockholder equity remaining flat. Profit margins rose from 4.2 percent to 7.0 percent (ABB Financial Analysis 2000). It is difficult to see any major transformation in ABB that could be directly attributable to the benchmarking of GE's best practices in either 1993 or 1999.

In January 2001, Goran Lindahl stepped down as CEO of ABB before his term was up, and Jorgen Centerman, former head of ABB's automation business, replaced him. Lindahl's public reason for stepping down was that ABB needed a CEO with the specific skills involved in moving the firm onto the Internet. He reaffirmed ABB's corporate vision to accelerate the firm's shift away from heavy industrial products and towards new technologies and services. Centerman immediately unveiled a new management team and a structural overhaul designed to accelerate this shift (Woodruff 2001, A6).

Goals

Centerman reaffirmed ABB's corporate goals to

- improve sales 6 to 7 percent a year to 2005,
- improve operating profit margins from 7 to 12 percent by 2003, and
- complete ABB's overhaul of its stock and accounting system and list the firm on the New York Stock Exchange by the second quarter of 2001.

Centerman added one new goal to this list, to

- upgrade ABB's information technology systems to world class.

Implementing Structures

In order to meet these goals, Centerman believed ABB must undertake several changes. First, it must restructure its outdated management system. Second, it must establish a new incubator division to cultivate new businesses and technologies. Third, it must establish a new corporate process division to implement common processes and group-wide infrastructures such as quality control, supply division management, e-business development, and information technology systems. Fourth, it must focus its product divisions on customer service for large businesses and industries.

ABB's new management structure is built around Four Customer focused divisions. Utilities; Oil, Gas and Petroleum; Process Industries and Manufacturing; and Customer Industries will each focus on providing products and service to customers. Two divisions—Power Technology Products and Automation Technology Products—will provide ABB inputs to the four customer focused divisions. Three divisions—Financial Services, New Vendors, and Computer Process—support organizational infrastructure repositioning.

In February of 2002, Jurgan Dormann replaced Percy Barnevik as chairman of the ABB board. Barnevik stepped down amid a crisis in confidence among stockholders of ABB's leadership. Two problems undergrid this crisis in confidence. First, in 1990, when Barnevik was chairman of the board and CEO, ABB acquired Combustion Engineering of Connecticut. In making this acquisition, ABB did not properly exercise due diligence in exploring the firm's strengths and weaknesses. By 2001, Combustion Engineering and in turn ABB had 94,000 asbestos civil lawsuits launched against the firm. Losses from these suits are projected to cost more than $2 billion. ABB later sold Combustion Engineering. However, ABB remained responsible for the liabilities from these suits. These liabilities did not become public until 2000 when ABB had to open its books in order to be listed on the New York Stock Exchange (Hall 2002, 28).

Second, two ABB CEOs retired from the firm in the last five years. When they retired, each received excessively large retirement packages. Barnevik and Lindahl received a total of $137 million. These two benefit packages were not reviewed by ABB's board of directors but were approved by the board chairman, Percy Barnevik. When Barnevik was forced to resign in 2001 by the board due to ABB's asbestos problems and these retirement packages, Jurgen Dormann, the new board chairman, discovered the retirement packages and publicly appealed to the two former CEOs to return portions of these retirement packages. In February of 2002, ABB negotiated the return of $82 million from the two CEOs (Woodruff 2002, A12).

Each of the above problems caused the investment community to lose confidence in ABB's top leadership. In addition, in January of 2002, ABB announced that a slowdown in the global economy would cause ABB's profits in 2001 to run $691 million in the red, down from

$1.4 billion in 2000. ABB stock prices dropped from $116 per share in 2000 to $7.15 in 2002 (Woodruff 2002, A12). ABB's new leadership team is now moving quickly to restructure the board, and the firm is undertaking to sell major portions of its financial services unit and to cut 12,000 jobs in an attempt to return the firm to profitability. All these problems are leading to a general breakdown in ABB's political top-down culture and may provide a climate for introducing significant changes rooted in their benchmarking of GE's best practices (Woodruff 2002, W1).

Conclusions Regarding Culture as a Limiting Factor in Benchmarking

90% of the firms leading their respective market segments in a Fortune *International 500 survey attribute major portions of their competitiveness to the benchmarking of best practices.*

(Obloj, Cushman and Kozminski, 1995:63)

Corporate cultures once internalized are difficult to change. They are an orientational system from which the most powerful and humble can borrow to give dignity, direction, and a sense of belonging to their lives. Cultures are restrictive: they provide a preferred viewpoint on life. Therefore it is not surprising that when a firm like ABB, with a strong top-down, conservative, slow decision-making culture benchmarks GE, with a strong bottom-up culture, innovative, rapid-response time, draws conclusions from its observations which support its own cultural perspective. Several conclusions follow from culture as a limiting factor.

First, the benchmarking firm failed to realize the importance of GE implementing structures which guaranteed supplier, worker, and customer inputs into the organizational decision-making process.

Second, the benchmarking process transformed conclusions from GE's culture in agreement with ABB's culture while praising GE's cultural differences.

Third, while ABB had the learning capability and long time line to implement GE's best practices, its corporate culture limited significantly its ability to see and then change its own culture in order to implement GE's best practices.

Fourth, repeated benchmarking of GE did not significantly alter ABB's effectiveness in operationalizing GE's best practices.

References

ABB. Com.Financial Facts.2000.

Andrews, E.L. (1997). ABB to cut 10,000 jobs in Europe and the U.S. *International Herald Tribune*, 1, October 22, 10.

Asea-Brown-Boveri (1988). *The Economist,* May 26, 19–22.

Berling, R. (1993). The emerging approach to business strategy: Building a relationship adventure. *Business Horizons*, July/August, 16.

Burt, T. (1999). All change for profit. *Financial Times*, June 29, 10.

Cushman, D. P. and King, S. S. (1994). A comparative study of communication within multinational organizations in the United States and Western Europe. In *Communication in Multinational Organizations, Annual of International and Intercultural Communication,* ed. R. Wiseman and Shuter, (vol. 18). Beverly Hills, Calif.: Sage.

————. (1997). The repositioning of Asea Brown and Boveri. *Focus on Change Management,* March, 11–16.

Fleming, C. (1999). ABB's chief rapidly rebuilds, gives European giant new power. *Wall Street Journal,* December 21, A18.

Gibson, M. (1995). How ABB became Europe's best. *The European,* October 11, 19.

Gutknecht, D. (1982). Conceptualizing culture in organizational theory. *California Sociologist* (winter): 68–87.

Hall, W. (2002). ABB takes asbestos claim charges. *Financial Times*, January 31, 28.

Harnischfeger, F., Von Der Wense, G., and Hagen, T. (1993). General Electric—A company for ABB to learn from? (ABB Internal Consulting Report), Mannheim, Germany. November 30.

Kapetein, J., Reed, W. Schares, G., Miles, C., Rossant, J., Rapoport, C. (1992). The torch Swede invades the U.S. *Fortune,* June 19, 76–79.

Kennedy, C. (1992). ABB: Model merger for the new Europe. *Long Range Planning* 25 (October): 30.

Kets de Vries, M. F. R. (1994). Making a giant dance. *Across the Board* (October): 27–32.

Misguided medicine (1998). *Financial Times,* August 13, 12.

Morris, R. (1999). ABB reorganized. *Forbes,* August 23, 61.

Obloj, K., Cushman, D. P., and Kozminski, A. (1995). *Continuous Improvement: Theory and Practice.* Albany: State University of New York Press.

Olson, E. (2002). ABB plans to sell part of its financial unit. *Wall Street Journal*, April 3, W1.

Olson, E. (2002). ABB expects to report loss over asbestos cases. *Wall Street Journal*, January 31, W1.

Shein, E. (1984). Coming to a new awareness of organizational culture. *Sloan Management Review* (winter): 3–11.

Taylor, W. (1991). The logic of global business: An interview with Percy Barnevik. *Harvard Business Review*, March/April 105.

Weaver, R. (1964). *Visions of Order: The Cultural Crises of Our Time*. Baton Rouge, La.: Louisiana University Press.

Welch, J. (1993). The speed and spirit of a boundaryless company. *GE Reports*, April 28, 1–4.

Woodruff, D. (2000). ABB makeover leads to jump in its earnings. *Wall Street Journal*, February 4, A12.

———. (2000). Alstom purchase of ABB stake in venture is plus for both firms. *Wall Street Journal*, April 3, A24.

———. (2001). New ABB chairman off to running start. *Wall Street Journal*, January 12, A16.

———. (2002). New ABB chief moves to restore group's credibility with investors. *Wall Street Journal*, February 25, A18.

———. (2002). Former CEOs of ABB reach deal on dispute over payment. *Wall Street Journal*, March 11, A12.

Part 3

The Significance of Benchmarking Backbone Communication Processes

Understanding the what of competitiveness is a prerequisite for catching up. Understanding the why of competitiveness is a prerequisite for getting out front.

(Mamal and Prahalad, 1993:76)

In **Part 3** we explore the significance of the backbone communication processes located in each of our four benchmarking studies undertaken in part 1. More specifically, we will explore the following:

(1) The use of firm *profiling by the Dell Computer Corporation to guide the content of effective interaction* with a firm's stakeholders.

(2) The use of the *stages involved in communication organizational change by GE's leaders* as a tool for creating organizational innovation and breakthroughs.

(3) The use of *linking marketing strategies to communication strategies by Microsoft* as a means of limiting competition while satisfying customer needs.

(4) The use of candor and future *strategies and opportunities by Monsanto* as a means of overcoming past problems in the effectively soliciting investor support.

9

Backbone Communication Processes in the Benchmarking of Best Practices: The Development of Organizational Communication Theory

The companies that find a way to engage every mind—harvest every volt of passionate energy—bring excitement to the lives of their people—and break every critical barrier between people—will be the companies that win in the '90s and beyond and we at GE intend to be the best of them.

(Jack Welch, 1993:1)

An organization's stakeholders consist of its management, workers, suppliers, investors, partners, and customers. What Jack Welch is suggesting in the above quotation is that in order to "harvest every volt of passionate energy," "engage every mind," and "bring excitement" to their lives, these stakeholders must be in active communication with each other, expressing their interests, concerns, and suggestions for improving organizational performance. In order for this to be accomplished, firms must break down the barriers between people and facilitate open expression and rapid decision making in regard to these interests, concerns, and suggestions. Welch argues that the organizations which do that will be the firms which win in the 1990s and beyond.

Our inquiry into the benchmarking of organizational communication best practices is at an end and it certainly confirms Welch's claims and illustrates how this can be accomplished in any firm. It is therefore time to take stock of these solutions and their significance in regard to what we have discovered and to integrate our findings into a coherent theory of organizational communication. Our stocktaking will be undertaken in three areas: (1) what we have learned from our benchmarking of commication best practices regarding the methodology for constructing communication theory; (2) what insights such an approach to theory suggests regarding the organizational communication processes; and (3) what substantive theory of organizational communication is provided by our inquiry.

Benchmarking Best Practices as a Methodology for Developing Communication Theory

Building general and specific theories of organizational communication has been hampered by several methodological problems. Organizations differ in structure, size, culture, industrial focus, markets, leadership styles, and learning skills. These differences make any type of cross-organizational generalizations regarding performance outcomes difficult. This inquiry has revealed several methodological processes for overcoming these problems.

First, a theorist can locate cross-organizational functions which anchor organizational communication processes. Three such functions are organizational strategies such as cycle time reduction, organizational communication processes such as leadership and producing annual reports, and a firm's customer processes such as marketing.

Second, a theorist can then locate reoccurring critical success factors for performing these functions. Three such critical success factors are (1) putting in place four rapid-response communication processes for linking a firm's stakeholders and decision makers, (2) putting in place a sequential organizational leadership strategy for linking a firm's competitive positioning to its internal processes and (3) strengthening its global reach, a linking system between investor concerns and the communication of organizational performance outcomes and future potential.

Third, a theorist can then specify the quantitative and qualitative targets which indicate the levels of performance which when achieved exceed the performance levels of one's competitors, thus establishing world-class performance standards. These standards can be adjusted upward as the learning and innovative capacity of one's own firm and its competitors improve.

Finally, a theorist can delineate the backbone communication processes which specify the content that communication processes must contain in order to meet the critical success factors and targets. Four such backbone communication processes are communication profiling, a motivational sequence for communicating the need to implement change, the linking of marketing strategies and communication strategies, and the linking of performance outcomes and future potential to investors' commitments and support. Important organizational communication theories emerge, as we have seen, from this location of cross-organizational functions, reoccuring critical success factors, the specificity of industry leading performance targets, and delineating the backbone communication processes necessary for meeting the targets and critical success factors.

Insights from This Approach to Developing Communication Theory

While as we have argued reducing the cycle time it takes to perform organizational activities does appear to improve organizational outcome measures, and the increased speed and effectiveness of communication does appear to be the most significant process for reducing cycle time, we seem to have learned something more about this general communication process.

First, the use of appropriate content in these rapid-response systems is controlled by the backbone communication processes which appear to be organizational-activity specific. These backbone communication processes are function specific, that is, leadership and marketing communication with stockholders. Even in the case of Dell, the profiling of communication intent varies by the linkage set up between organizational decision makers and customers, suppliers, workers, and continuous-improvement teams. However, in each case the content employed is designed to speed effective organizational performance.

Second, the means for communicating content may vary from the Internet in the case of Dell, to face-to-face interaction in the case of GE's rapid-response system; however, the content of that interaction to be significant is dictated by the functional processes being employed, that is, leadership, marketing, and so forth.

Third, it is very clear that there is an important linkage at each level of organizational function between the organizational strategy being employed and the interpretation of the appropriate action to be taken from the functional content employed. All of the categories employed in benchmarking Dell, and indicating the effects of Dell's use of the interaction on its competitors, reveal a speed-to-market strategy, and thus all the backbone communication profiling is interpreted as effective on organizational outcome measures primarily in terms of the speed-to-market strategy. The developing of organizational leaders who perform well is again tied to the strategies of positioning a firm in high-growth, high-profit areas, developing a firm's internal structure to support that vision, and extending a firm's records to the global market to bring about that vision. The backbone communication processes employed—demonstrating a threat that requires a firm to change, a vision and set of targets to guide the change, creating attention and then releasing it to appropriately motivate the change, and empowering point people to lead each aspect of the change—are given significance by reorienting organizational activity in terms of the original strategies employed.

It is because of the consistency of organizational findings across different types of firms, markets, customers, and so forth that general and specific theories of organizational communication must be rooted in these functions. It is because the appropriate content of communication and form vary by organizational function that the backbone communication processes are general by organizational function. Finally, it is because a firm's general and specific functions and backbone communication processes are integrated in terms of the various organizational strategies being employed that we must include those principles of interpretation in our theory formation. This then is the structure and content of effective organizational communication and the principles of interpretation to be employed.

The Substantive Organizational Communication Theory Which Emerges from Our Inquiry

The benchmarking of high-speed management at Dell revealed the use of four rapid-response communication systems between an organization and its stakeholders. Rapid-response systems were constructed by Dell, employing the Internet between (1) marketing, sales, and the customers; (2) customers, management, and Dell's suppliers, manufacturers, and distributors of products; (3) customers and Dell's service system; and (4) management and the customers, suppliers, manufacturers, distributors, and maintenance staff involved in continuous-improvement programs. These interactive rapid-response systems represent the critical success factors for achieving Dell's world-class performance. Targets were then set for speed of response and quality of performance in each of these rapid-response relationships, which allowed Dell to significantly outperform its competitors. These included orders taken and payment received within one day, supplier's parts delivered within 15 minutes, computers assembled within 3 hours, products delivered within 3 days, and a continuous-improvement program that improves performance 20 percent a year.

These four Internet rapid-response systems set up the structure of the communication processes involved, and the targets indicated the appropriate levels of speed necessary to outperform competitors. However, they say little about the appropriate content involved in these communication processes. The backbone communication processes necessary for determining the appropriate content of interaction were developed through customer, product, value chain, maintenance, and continuous-improvement profiling. In each of these types of profiling, content is gathered. For example, *customer profiling* allows Dell to track the number, type, and configuration of computers ordered so that customer preferences can be discussed and systems updated when the technology changes, and so forth. *Product profiling* allows Dell to aggregate all customer orders in such a manner as to anticipate parts orders, sales patterns, and component usage. *Value chain profiling* allows Dell to issue report cards to each segment in the value chain on performance time, product quality, work left unfinished, and most common maintenance and distribution problems. *Continuous-improvement profiling* allows Dell to track stakeholders' primary concerns and suggested innovations and to share that information with all team members.

The significance of profiling is most apparent in setting the agenda for and controlling the content of interaction between Dell and its stakeholders. Profiling assures that the content of interaction is responsive to all the stakeholders' needs while focusing on improved organizational performance. This in turn creates satisfied and involved stakeholders. For example, profiling contributes to the development and use of new value chain modifications, to setting up Internet chatrooms by content areas of concern to all stakeholders, to selecting the content for Dell Talk, the online management/customer interaction show, to selecting the problem/solutions discussed on Ask Dudly, Dell's online advanced AI maintenance program, and to designing My Dell, the online Web page customization show. In short, the backbone communication processes involved in profiling are necessary agenda-setting mechanisms for addressing the concerns of all Dell's stakeholders in such a manner as to achieve stakeholder satisfaction, improved performance, effective continuous improvement, and reduced cycle time.

A Leadership Communication Sequence for Motivating Change at the General Electric Corporation

The benchmarking of organizational leadership located three critical success factors involved in effectively leading a firm: (1) the positioning of a firm's businesses in high-growth, high-margin markets, where the firm has the capability of gaining significant market shares; (2) the development of organizational infrastructure, that is, corporate culture, rapid-response communication systems, and continuous-improvement systems, to establish and maintain a lead over competitors in organizational performance; and (3) then expanding a firm's market penetration into the global economy. To accomplish these three stages of organizational development, a leader must set quantitative and qualitative targets which are clear and appropriate for outperforming the competitors in all areas of a firm's performance. However, once again critical success factors and targets set up the structure of communication but say very little regarding the content of communication or how a leader is to motivate successful performance.

Here again a backbone communication process emerged during our benchmarking efforts which provided just such a motivational content. Across all three transformations Welch employed a common sequence of motivational communication which unfolded in six stages:

(1) ***A significant perceived threat to GE.*** In the *first* transformation it was the threat from Japan Inc. In the *second* it was the rising entrepreneurial spirit of firms in Europe and in Asia and the need to think like a large firm but act like a small firm. In the *third* transformation it was slow growth in the major global markets and GE's own excellence in performance.

(2) ***A vision of how to confront these threats.*** The *first* transformation was to be "the most productive and valued firm in the world." The *second* was to be a "boundaryless firm through speed, simplicity and self confidence." The *third* was to be a "multipolar, multicultural, Internet service firm."

(3) *A set of quantitative and qualitative targets aimed at achieving that vision.* The *first* transformation targets were to be 1 or 2 in market shares and to raise sales, profits, quality, inventory turns, income from new products, income from exports, and stockholder return. The targets in the *second* transformation were to raise all the previous targets and create a new corporate culture, communication system, and continuous-improvement system. In the *third* transformation, the targets were to be 1 or 2 in each major market in the global economy, to create e-business centers, investments and training into Europe and Asia, to move the firm's 12 businesses to the Internet, and to make 70 percent of sales from service areas.

(4) *Put in place a set of state-of-the-art implementing structures for creating and releasing the functions necessary to motivate change.* In the *first* transformation, it was cutting 150 businesses to 12 in which GE could be 1 or 2 in markets shares in high-growth, high-margin businesses. Also 150,000 workers were laid off, 11 of 12 business heads were replaced, and 9 layers of management were cut to 5, while several old businesses were sold and several new ones purchased. In the *second*, a new corporate culture, a new four-level communication system, and a new continuous-improvement program were put in place. In the *third* transformation, a Six Sigma Quality program, business centers in Europe and Asia, training programs for Europe and Asia, Smart Bombing investments, and Internet business processes were put in place.

It is GE's unique skill in creating and releasing a tension in a positive manner which sets it apart from other high-performance firms. Pressure is created for change by creating some major tension in the firm, then putting in place the appropriate implementing structures to motivate the solution and targets which can release the tension, and backing that solution quickly with resources, training, and point people, while adjusting the bonus and promotion systems to reward change. The creativity, precision, and breakthrough thinking which goes into these implementing structures is why GE is among the most frequently benchmarked firms in the world.

(5) *The empowerment of people to lead and participate in the change.* In the *first* transformation, empowerment was

achieved by cutting 9 layers of management to 5, putting in place 12 new businesses and their leaders and workers. In the *second*, it was the creation of a self-actualizing culture, the restructuring of communication between managers, customers, workers, and stakeholders as well as the focused communication caused by workout and its four types of teamwork. In the *third*, it was the empowerment of Internet and service teams.

(6) ***Begin the process of change again.*** This established a culture which looks forward to and profits from continuous organizational change.

These backbone communication processes provided the content necessary for motivating significant organizational performance. In ABB's 1999 benchmarking of GE's superior organizational performance, the benchmarking team concluded that GE had developed a culture of change, one which searched out opportunities for breakthroughs in every aspect of organizational performance, from product development, to corporate culture, to a rapid-response system and quality control. They concluded that "error management, coupled with an appetite for risk and innovation are the essential factors for a breakthrough conducive environment" and that such breakthroughs were necessary for the sustained growth in organizational performance achieved by GE (Burt 1999, 6). This then is the significance of GE's backbone motivational leadership communication processes. It creates a sustained growth in organizational performance rooted in an entrepreneurial and controlled risk-taking culture which sought out and exploited opportunities in every area of organizational activity in order to create breakthrough change.

Linking Marketing and Communication Strategies at the Microsoft Software Company

The benchmarking of organizational marketing at Microsoft revealed five critical success factors: (1) entering evolving mass markets early or stimulating new markets with good products which can become the industrial standard; (2) incrementally continuously improving products making old products obsolete; (3) pushing volume sales to ensure that products become and remain the industry standard; (4) leveraging the industry standard to develop new products and market linkages; and (5) integrating, extending, and simplifying products and services to reach new mass markets. Targets were then set in each product and service market for achieving the critical success factors.

Once again a set of backbone communication processes emerged for determining the content which communication must present if these critical success factors and targets are to be achieved. These involve the linkages between four communication strategies and four market performance outcomes.

(1) *Linking Microsoft's unique brand of teamwork to its product development and continuous improvement processes.* Microsoft's unique brand of teamwork weights product development teams in favor of being responsive to pent-up customer demand. This forces product development to respond to emerging mass market demand. For example, in 1999 Windows NT held 38 percent of the server market, Linux 25 percent, NetWare 19 percent, and Unix 15 percent. In order to develop a mass market Microsoft had to extend its data center software beyond NT to the other three markets.

In late 1999, Microsoft responded to this consumer demand with three key moves. *First*, it developed the concept of Internet utilities, stand-alone programs which have the option of using the Windows operating system or not. Such Internet utilities would be server-based operating systems which integrated a variety of programs for a common purpose. The data-centered program could integrate back office suite, a suite of value-chain integration programs, a suite of data storage programs, and a suite of supplier bazaar programs into a single data management operating system. *Second*, this data center utility would employ XML as a programming language. XML is an Internet standard intended to integrate content, financial information, and transactions in a manner suitable for use on Windows NT, Linux, NetWare, and Unix, thus extending Microsoft's reach into its new markets for database software. *Third*, to install and adapt this software to the specific needs of various businesses, Microsoft needed to create a new, large, and competent service division such as those employed by Oracle, IBM, and Sun Microsystems. All of this was done and will be reflected in Windows 2000 for data centers which was released in November 2000 (Markoff 2000:B1).

(2) ***Linking Microsoft's unique acquisition and alliance policies to mass market product development.*** While Microsoft was desperately in need of a service division in order to compete with Oracle, IBM, and Sun Microsystems in the server and data center market, it realized that constructing such a division quickly would be a serious problem. In March of 2000, Microsoft formed an alliance with Anderson Consulting to create a 5,000 employee technology service firm for that purpose. The new service firm is valued at $1 billion. In addition the new firm will give specialized instructions in Microsoft products to 25,000 other Anderson Consulting employees, some 3,000 of whom develop complex business applications and can now do so employing Microsoft technology (Clark 2000, A3). This alliance, along with Windows 2000 for data centers, will help close the gap between Microsoft and Oracle, IBM, and Sun Microsystems in the creation of both large and small databases. In addition, Microsoft has $19 billion in cash for future investments in acquisitions and alliances if needed.

(3) ***Linking competitive pricing, exclusive contracts, and software bundling to volume marketing and distribution of Microsoft products.*** Microsoft is and will continue to be the low-cost high-quality provider of database software. Its products have been and are priced to be about one-third the cost of Oracle and IBM products. Microsoft's exclusive service contract with Anderson Consulting creates a 5,000 person service firm. Microsoft 2000 for data centers bundles back office suite, a value chain suite, a data storage suite, and Windows operating system into a data center operating system. SAP bundles Microsoft 2000 with its business-to-customer and business-to-business software packages. Microsoft bundles data center software into its back office suite.

(4) ***The leveraging of software standards to limit competitors' sales in new mass markets.*** Until now Windows NT, the dominant software in the server market, has been hampered by three problems: its reliability, its ability to link with Unix, Linux, and NetWare servers, and its ability to expand to any level of size and complexity. The appearance of Windows 2000 Datacenter will resolve all these problems. This, along with its new Anderson Consulting division, led experts to predict that Windows 2000

Datacenter and Windows NT with its price, bundling, and service advantages, will move from 38 percent to 50 percent of the server market by 2001 (Clark 2000, A3). Already the Boeing Corporation has asked Microsoft to create its business to business Web site leaving Oracle in favor of a more cost efficient system (Gomes and Cole 2000, B2). If such migrations continue, Microsoft's position in the data center market should dramatically improve.

Finally, it is significant that Microsoft's utilities strategy of software bundling employs XML, an open programming language for the Internet. This change removes most of the objections raised by the government in its antitrust trial of Microsoft. In so doing Microsoft moves forward, still employing its world-class marketing strategy linked to its four communication content strategies while increasing its growth and maintaining its 50 percent profit margins and competitive edge.

Effectively Communicating with Investors at the Monsanto Company

The benchmarking of annual reports at Monsanto revealed three critical success factors. Such reports must address up front (1) current sales, profit, stockholder value, operating margins, and one-time charges against profits, as well as future expectations in each of these areas; (2) future strategic directions and leadership changes; and (3) the current and future performance of key products and services. The targets to be employed in creating instant comprehension of the reports were (1) the selection, repetition, and variation on a common set of themes; (2) placing these themes in a clear deductive format; and (3) illustrating all key themes with simple, bright-colored visuals such as bar charts and contribution pies.

Once again a set of four backbone communication processes emerged for meeting targets and achieving the critical success factors:

(1) *The use of a chairperson's or CEO's letter to highlight future expectations and current results.* Top management has to lead new initiatives by backing them with resources, putting in place implementing structures and monitoring mechanisms, and designating the appropriate point people to champion the change. This letter is designed to demonstrate that all of these factors are addressed by top management in the appropriate manner so as to make future expectations realizable.

(2) **The handling of negative information up front in a candid manner.** When management is up front and candid about bad news, that creates an impression of honesty. When management puts in place a carefully monitored correction so that the bad news will not occur again, that creates a feeling of trust on the part of investors. This followed by an example of what management has learned from the problem and the future benefits of the correction creates a feeling of respect for management on the part of investors.

(3) **A focus on future expectations and the specific plans made to make sure these expectations are met.** Once again indicating the commitment of adequate resources, clear implementing structures, accomplished point people, and careful monitoring procedures creates a feeling of high reliability among investors in management in meeting future expectations.

(4) **A discussion of new strategies and business processes for increasing a firm's competitiveness.** Knowledgeable investors are aware of market contingencies and competitors' capability. This invites management to outline strategies and business processes which can make opportunities out of market contingencies and create new business models for neutralizing competitors' capabilities.

Taken collectively these four backbone communication processes for annual reports build confidence in a firm's management. They do so by creating a feeling of honesty, trust, and respect for management's method of dealing with bad news by focusing on future expectations and specific plans for success, and by outlining the specific strategies and business models which will take advantage of market contingencies and neutralize competitors' capabilities in responding to management's plans.

This then is the significance of our four backbone communication processes which our benchmarking studies of Dell, GE, Microsoft, and Monsanto best practices revealed as necessary for motivating world class performance.

Profiling was a necessary agenda setting mechanism for guiding interaction in such a manner as to address stakeholder concerns. Addressing stakeholder concerns in turn created stakeholder satisfaction, improved organizational performance, created effective continuous improvement, and significantly reduced a firm's cycle time in getting its products and services to market.

A leadership communication sequence for motivating change was necessary for developing a culture of change which was entrepreneurial in character and risk controlled in outcomes. Such a sequence created an organizational culture which sought out opportunities for breakthrough performance in every aspect of organizational activity, which was essential for creating sustained organizational growth.

Linking marketing and communication strategies was necessary for creating market domination, high margins, and increased growth. Such linkages, when properly constructed, limit competitive access to markets in such a manner as to eliminate them from serious competition.

Annual reports which effectively communicate with investors are necessary for management to demonstrate honesty and build trust and respect while focusing on the future plans, products, and services as well as strategies and business models which take advantage of market contingencies and neutralize competitor capabilities. This in turn generates greater stockholder confidence in management and greater market capitalization.

Our inquiry as planned has come to a stopping place. We have explicated the critical success factors, performance targets, and backbone communication processes involved in developing a world-class (1) High-Speed Management communication system, (2) leadership communication system, (3) marketing communication system, and (4) annual report communication system. Organizations which aspire to world-class levels of performance will need to examine these best practices carefully if they are to compete more effectively in the global economy. We have thus completed our inquiry into the what and why of excellence in organizational communication performance.

References

Burt, T. (1999). All change for profits. *Financial Times*, June 29, 10.

Clark, D. K. (2000). Microsoft sets an alliance with Anderson. *Wall Street Journal*, March 12, A3.

Gomes, L., and Cole, J. (2000). Microsoft moves into business to business. *Wall Street Journal*, March 29, B2.

Markoff, J. (2000). Microsoft plans a new strategy for the Internet. *New York Times*, April 8, B1.

Welch, J. (1993). The speed and spirit of a boundaryless company. *GE Speech Reprints*, April 28, 1–4.

Index